For M.

with _____ng & love,

Emily

Night of the Broken Glass

and

Transformations

Also by EMILY BORENSTEIN

BOOKS

Cancer Queen (Barlenmir House, 1979)
Night of the Broken Glass (Timberline Press, 1981)

CHAPBOOKS

Woman Chopping (Timberline Press, 1978)
Finding My Face (Thunder City Press, 1979)
From a Collector's Garden (Timberline Press, 2001)

NIGHT
OF
THE BROKEN GLASS

and

TRANSFORMATIONS

Emily Borenstein

TIMBERLINE PRESS
Fulton, Missouri
2007

This book is set in Calisto MT. Book design by Clarence
Wolfshohl.
Portrait of Emily Borenstein on back cover is by
Cynthia Harris-Pagano (artist).

ISBN 978-0-944048-40-5

Timberline Press
6281 Red Bud
Fulton, Missouri 65251
www.timberlinepress.com

ACKNOWLEDGMENTS

Grateful acknowledgement is made to the following magazines in which some of these poems were first published: *American Jewish Times Outlook*, *A Shout In The Street* (Queens College), *Bitterroot*, *Connections*, *Cumberlands* (Pikeville College), *Cyclo-Flame*, *En Passant/Poetry*, *Epos*, *European Judaism* (England), *Friede Uber Israel* (West Germany), *Glassworks*, *Gourmet Magazine*, *Home Planet News*, *Israel Horizons* (Israel), *Jewish Currents*, *Long Shot*, *Mikrokosmos* (Wichita State U), *Mundus Artium*, *Pivot* (State College, Pa.), *Poetica*, *Poet Lore*, *Pontchartrain Review*, *M'godolim*, *Poetry Venture*, *Response*, *Spafaswap*, *State And Mind*, *Studia Mystica* (California State U), *Telephone*, *The Greenfield Review*, *The Jewish Spectator*, *The Other*, *The Remington Review*, *The Rufus*, *Tree*, *Twigs* (Pikeville College), *Uroboros*, *Visions*, *Voices- Israel* (Israel), *Voices Of The Seventies*, *Waves* (York U, Canada), *Wind Magazine*, *Webster Review* (Webster College), and *Zahir*.

Anthologies that include some of the poems in this book are *Anthology of Magazine Verse 1981, Blood To Remember: American Poets on the Holocaust* published by Texas Tech University Press (1991)edited by Charles Fishman; *Emerson Of Harvard* published by Quill Press (2003) edited by John H. Morgan; *Voices Within The Ark: The Modern Jewish Poets* published by Pushcart Press, co-published with Avon Books in 1980 and edited by Howard Schwartz & Anthony Rudolph; *Images From The Holocaust: A Literature Anthology*, NTC Publishing (1996) . Poems of mine have also appeared in the anthologies *Phoenix Rising: Contemporary Jewish Voices* published in 1981 by Micah Publications, edited by Roberta Kalechofsky, and the anthology *September11,2001: American Writers Respond* published by Etruscan Press in 2002 and edited by William Heyen in which four of my "Twelve Meditations for September 11, 2001" appeared.

Four of the poems in this book first appeared in *Cancer Queen*.

Heartfelt gratitude to Morris, my husband, for his devotion, love and quiet support. He is a steady anchor in my life and helped to make the completion of this book, in ways large and small, a reality.

A very special thank you to my daughter Rachel for her patience, clarity of thought and attention to detail that were an invaluable help to me in editing this book. Her patience and enthusiasm surpassed my wildest hopes.

My thanks to Rabbi Joel and Aviva Schwab for their advice on religious references in some of the poems in this book.

My deep appreciation to Clarence Wolfshohl, publisher of Timberline Press, for bringing out this edition of *Night of the Broken Glass/Transformations*, as well as *Night Of The Broken Glass* in 1981 in an edition of 500 and two of my chapbooks, *Woman Chopping* in 1978 and *From A Collector's Garden* in 2001. Clarence designed the artistic serigraphs and linoleum block designs that grace the first two books and the artistic drawings in *A Collector's Garden*. All three books were hand printed by Clarence for Timberline Press. I also thank Patricia Wolfshohl for her excellent work in formatting my book for the printer.

Dedicated to my husband,
and children,
grandchildren and great-grandchild
and to the memory of my parents and brother
and all my relatives who died
in the Holocaust

TABLE OF CONTENTS

NIGHT OF THE BROKEN GLASS

OUT OF THE ASHES

Out Of The Ashes   23

I MUST TELL THE STORY

I Must Tell The Story   27
Raoul Wallenberg, Missing Hero Of The Holocaust 28
Verdi's Requiem Played And Sung By Jews
    In Terezin Concentration Camp, Summer—1944 34

GHETTOS

After Germany Made Hitler Its Savior   41
Mourning   43
Night Of The Broken Glass   44
The Shoah (Whirlwind-Holocaust)   46
Rhapsody   48
Blind Wall   50
Atrocities   51
Dancing And Singing   52
In This Passover Season   53
Like Sparrows Shivering   54
Hear This   55
The Death Pits At Ponery   56
Menorah   57
Efforts To Save The Children   58
House Of Death   59
Escape Through The Sewers   60
Uprising In The Warsaw Ghetto   62
Contempt For Death   63
Women Of Valor   64
There Shall Be Time No Longer   65

DEPORTATIONS

A Wheel Of Fortune With Razor-Sharp Knives 69
Night Journey To Poland 70
Holocaust 71
The Children Must Be Deported 72
The Children Must Not Be Forgotten 73
Father Of Orphaned Children 74
Jews, Step Forward 75
Massacre 76
Arrivals And Departures 77
Conflagration 78
The Last Words Spoken 79

THE DEATH CAMPS

In The World Of Suffering And Death 83
The Excavator 84
Death Jew 85
Stones, Collect Stones 86
Mauthausen 87
Everything Leads To The Stoves 89
They Fought Back 90

IN THE SHADOW OF THE HOLOCAUST

Remembering Bells Ringing In Kishinev 93
His Hands Wept 94
The Silent Ones 95
What Is It All About? 96
Who Was Anna Wachalska? 97
The Survivors 98
Triumph Of The Dead 99
A Visit To Auschwitz 100
Jew Dolls 101

SONG OF THE RETURN

Ascent 105
Uniting Dreams And Reality In Israel 106
Israel Of All Generations 107

Intoxications Of Divinity   108
The Song Of The Return   109
Psalm Of Hope   111
Hope And Redemption   112
Ever-Present In My Life   114

TRANSFORMATIONS

TRANSFORMATIONS

A Share In The World To Come   119
Transformations   120
I Found The Key To A Holy Place   122
On The Day Of Atonement   124
I Turned The Pages Of A Book On The Life
    Of A Poet   126
A Soul On Fire   128
The Journey Upward And Inward   129

HOPE AND REDEMPTION

Begin This Day   133
Shofar-Blower   134
The Redeemer   135
Ungraspable Reality   137
The Legacy   138
Can A Fig Grow?   139
The Strength To Endure   140
Climbing   141
Divine Threads   142

QUESTIONING GOD

What God Is This Who Eludes Revelation And
    Communication?   145
What If God's Fingers Are Limp And Unwilling?   147
Why Does God Refuse To Reveal Her Being?   148
Reflections On The Ninth Day Of Av   149
The Fingerprints Of Dark Energy   150

Who Will Save The Branches Of The Tree Of Life
   From Destruction?   151
The Quantum Physicist And God   152
Spiritual Canticle   154
Binah (Understanding)   155
Through The Half-Opened Windows Of Life In
   Jeopardy   156
Who Mapped The Stars?   157

THE ILLUMINATED JOURNEY

Tearing Yourself Loose   161
Breakthrough   162
Rafting Up Passion River   163
World's End   164
Change   165
The Sea Is Thundering In A White Maelstrom   166
The Illuminated Journey   167
You Cannot Turn Back   168
An Ancient City Is There In My Dreams   169
It Is Difficult To Take The Journey Alone   170

MEDITATIONS

I Think Of You   173
The Sabbath Bride Is A Laughing Girl   174
Notes Trickle From My Fingers   175
The Day Of Judgment Lays Bare   176
The Light Streams Out   177
Truth In The Exilic Mode   178
Truth In The Rhapsodic Mode   179
Truth In The Midrashic Mode   180
Truth In The Mode Of Psychology And Intuition   182
A Blue Scroll Unwinding   184
Life Of The Letters   185
Psalm Of Thanksgiving   186
God Of Perpetuity, If You Should Call Me   187
In The Grandeur Of Evolution   188
Remember The Light   189
Come, My Beloved   190
Beyond Flesh To Flesh Coupling   191

Opening A Line Of Communication   192
Forgiveness And Understanding   193
I Give Thanks   194
Bearing Fruit   195
Transformed Into A Book Of Love   196
Root Of All Roots   197
The Clouds Are Walking   198
Full Of The Flight Of Birds   199
The Spirit Of Love Flows Everywhere   200
Nameless Petals   201

REFLECTIONS

A Sign Points To The Sinagogia   205
Where Is That Place, Shackled To The Moon   209
I Am Holding Fast To An Insubstantial Moment   211
In The Attic Of My Darkness   212
Riding The Death Car   213
The Messiah Of Death   214
Requiem For A Vanished Dream   215
Requiem For A Vanished Place   216
Firmly Rooted In The Divine Spirit   217
A Bush Aflame   218
The Universe Is A Massive, Monumental Poem   219
The Cosmic Gaze Inward   220
The Ubiquitous Muse   221
Parchments and Torah Skins   223
The Hebrew Letters Of The Alphabet   224
The Hourglass   225
The Letters Of The Alphabet Of Love   226
Profoundly Connected   227
Remaining Steadfast   228
The Moon Is A Leaden Ball   229
What Would Beethoven Have Said?   230
Hollowed Out By Chisels Of Fire   231
The World's Birthday   232
As The Sun Is Reduced To A Cinder   233
The Man Without Any Skin   234
In A Cave At The Mouth Of The Sea of Reeds   236
Many Threads   237
On The Death Of My Brother   238

From The Book Of Anticipations   239
Great Women In The Old Testament   240

OCTOBER SONG

Rebirth Of The Garden   245
The Flowers Come Alive At Night   246
Near The Limits Of Hearing   247
The Garden Is Steeped In The Perfume Of
    Old Roses   248
The Fires Of Mid-October Are Breaking Out   249
October Song   250
In Late October There Comes An End To Riotous
    Color   251
Work In The Garden Is Never Completed   252

MISCELLANEOUS

What Is There To Say About The Way Time
    Uses Me?   255
A Single Word Open To Chance   256
Thoughts Of A Red Empress In The Laotse-
    Chuangtse Era Based On Her Experiences   257
Meditation On A Quiet Night   258
Appassionato   259
Appassionata Sonata   260
The Bitterness Of Time   261
Old Woman In The Doctor's Office   262
Who Will Believe This?   263
Helfgott in Avery Fisher Hall   264
To The Falconer   265
Swimming Upstream   266
Baby Seal Harvest   267
In The Year 3000 A.D.   268
Stone Thoughts   269
The Villagers' Story
    (Sar Cheshma, Afghanistan 10/96)   270
Someone Else's Son Rocks Silently   272
How Many Dark And Desperate Days Of
    Downpour   273
In The Cities And Mountains Of Iraq   274

A Long Time Ago, A Faraway Country Doomed
    Itself   276

NOTES   278

NIGHT
OF
THE BROKEN GLASS

The walls filled with faces:
      holes
filled with hearts that had been condemned and torn
      down.
I walked with them: it was only in that chorus
that my voice refound the solitudes
where it was born.

Neruda

I am cut through
with rails,
pierced
by words,
by bullets,
churned up
by striding ploughshares,
hammers pound in me
and lips whisper,
and ships howl,
and birds call,
and groaning and singing
fill me,
louder in that mockery of silence.

No silence,
no more silence.

Veselin Khanchev

SUMMONS TO SURVIVAL

On the first Seder night in April, 1943, the Jews in the Warsaw Ghetto took up arms against their Nazi oppressors. It was the beginning of an epic battle--not for victory, as the resistance fighters knew from the outset, but for the honor of their people. On the walls of the Ghetto they posted an Eleventh Commandment: "Thou shalt not despair." It was their watchword and their legacy.

When the battle was near its end, the few Jews who still survived issued an appeal to their brethren around the world: "Remember us! Do not forget what we have suffered at the hands of our murderous enemy! Let our departure from the world in ashes and smoke not be in vain!"

In the Ghettos, survival, itself, was a form of resistance. Retaining some measure of human dignity against all odds was a form of resistance--organizing and maintaining underground schools and a medical school to train aspiring physicians, aiding the injured and the medically endangered, keeping up religious observance--all of these were acts of spiritual and moral resistance.

The Final Solution of Hitler and the Nazis was to exterminate every Jew on the face of the earth. For all their exterminations of Jews by every means possible, the Jews as a people live on as they have through millennia of expulsion, torture and death.

OUT OF THE ASHES

OUT OF THE ASHES

I am living in a world of torture and terror,
falling into a pit of horrors,
half-buried in the ashes of Jews who
were murdered by the Nazis.
I, who was born in America, write
these poems
with a pen dipped in ink
mixed with the blood and ashes of
Jews who died in the Holocaust.
The chimneys' flames are choked with
smoke.
All is nightmare under a flaming sky.
Wearing faces of stone,
the heartless cry,
"We could not help them."
They still choose not to remember.
Said the Ba'al Shem Tov:
*"In remembrance lies the secret of
redemption."*
People carry the shame of the past
into the future.
I rake the ashes of my own grief
that the world stood by
and did nothing.

I MUST TELL THE STORY

I MUST TELL THE STORY

I press my face to the pane of death to witness
the slaughter of Jews in Warsaw.
I must tell the story of this tragic event.
I write for my friend Pesha.
I write for cousin Perelke who was a comedic
actress
for my nephew Wiernicka who wrote poetry
for Chaim Kaplan and his "Scroll of Agony"
for half-witted Nathan who was hanged from
a tree
for Hinda, the bride, who died in her husband's
arms
for Motl, the tailor
for Bruno Schulz, his stories, his dreams
for Emmanuel Ringelblum who preserved for
posterity
the record of the slaughter.
Names pile up like pebbles on tombstones.
To forget you is to let you die twice.
To forget you is to hear in my head
the tormented notes of the Shofar calling me
from the houses of the dead.

RAOUL WALLENBERG, MISSING HERO OF THE HOLOCAUST

He was born into a family of wealth,
aristocracy and influence,
a descendent of a family of bankers
and owners of businesses in Sweden
with connections abroad.
As a young man in this rich and influential
family
he lived life in a charmed circle of
pretty girls
and bands playing Viennese waltzes,
not a care in the world,
his life a garden of roses properly pruned
and trained
and peonies full of promise--
a garden studded with fountains and
flowers the color of red wine
and stone angels looking over the lily pads,
a garden in which life emerged in bright
sunlight
with a feeling of permanence and repose.

Under the garden a little stream rose
and flowed out to sea,
its summer song full of dry thunder.
As his eyes followed the ominous gray
of the sky
dark thunder clouds gathered over
Europe.
The little stream became a surging river
speeding headlong,
full of challenges,
calling him to adventure and self-fulfillment.

His family history revealed that he was
one-sixteenth Jewish
with a clear and original mind and boundless

energy
His father was the Swedish ambassador
to Turkey.
His great-great grandfather on his mother's side
was born a Jew
who converted to the Lutheran faith.
He was so very proud of his partly Jewish
ancestry
that he remarked to a friend:
"A person like me, who is both a Wallenberg
and half-Jewish, can never be defeated."
Of course, his half-Jewish identity was an
exaggeration
and an example of how deeply he identified
with Jews.

Wallenberg was intensely likeable, courageous
and vital.
Away from the pleasures he enjoyed in life
he was increasingly aware of the plight of
Hungarian Jews shipped to death camps.
Little did he know in 1933 when he worked
at the Swedish Pavilion at the Chicago
World's Fair
and received his degree in architecture
at the University of Michigan in Ann Arbor
that fate would empower him to be the one who,
single-handedly,
would carry out one of the great humanitarian
rescues of imperiled Jews in modern history.
It was a dangerous mission
and a daring undertaking for anyone,
especially for a young man with no political
experience.

At first Swedish government officials thought
he was temperamentally unfit for such a job,
too young for so much responsibility
but they soon recognized
that indeed he had the fire in the belly

to be capable of rescuing thousands of Jews
from certain death.
He was bored with the lack of challenge in his
life
before he received this special assignment,
his energy and talent wasted on goose breasts,
pickled cucumbers and smoked salmon,
the staples in his successful import-export
business.

It is not beyond the realm of possibility how
his arrest by the Russian authorities
could have taken place in the paranoid world
of heavy-handed dictatorship
but to arrest him and imprison him for scores
of years
with no evidence of his spying on Russia!
Unthinkable! Historians credit him with rescuing
ten thousand Jews from mass extermination, but
Communist leaders in Russia could not believe
any sane man would risk his own life
to save the lives of Jews
unless he was a spy or a lunatic.

Raoul Wallenberg, missing hero of the Holocaust,
you are dead now after years and years of
incarceration, a political prisoner in Russia.
But who's to say if you're dead or alive?
Perhaps you're in your late 90's,
even 100 years old.
How and why did this happen?
The world has turned a blind eye to your plight,
to your imprisonment since the 1940's
because you regarded it as your sacred duty
and your mission in life
to save Jewish lives.
Was there no moral obligation to free you
from false charges
during the reign of the League of Nations
and today in the United Nations?

Does no one care about justice and truth
and the concern to do what is morally right?
Justice hangs her head in shame.

New bridges leap rivers in the Soviet Union,
new buildings are erected,
church bells ring out again in Russia,
the flowers sing.
The iron curtain was torn down but where *are* you,
Raoul Wallenberg?
There were sightings of you in Russian prisons
over the years.
You are one of the courageous heroes of
the Holocaust
whose only crime was rescuing
thousands of Hungarian Jews.

You set up hospitals, nurseries and soup kitchens,
issued Swedish passports and printed your own
special passports to save Jews even as they boarded
the cattle cars.
You stated to a friend, without grandstanding,
"I have a mission to save the Jewish nation!"
You personally intervened to rescue Jews.
You traveled the road between Budapest and
Hegyeshalom
with vanloads of food, medicine and warm clothes.
The sides of the road were full of the dead bodies of
Jews who died on this death march.

How is it possible that you were incarcerated
for life
for your bold and brave acts of goodness
and heroism
while the morbid sound of the wind full of regrets
still blows in blue skies
over Europe, Russia and America?

There were additional sightings of you by an
ex-prisoner in Vadivodo Camp near the Siberian city

of Irkutsk in 1967-68 and other sightings
including one in Lubianka Prison
for political prisoners, traitors and foreign spies
and by an ex-prisoner in Butyrka Prison.
The unanswered questions about your disappearance
remain unanswered.
Why did Russian authorities never let you go?
Why did they never admit they were wrong
to hold you on charges of spying?
Where is justice for you?

Why are voices not raised to plead your case
in the world court
to clear your name even if you died
persistently defiant to the end--
at peace with yourself.
What happened to you, Raoul Wallenberg,
savior of Hungarian Jews during World War II?
Did the Great Bear claw you to death slowly
or murder you outright?
Why didn't the world's leaders use political
pressure to obtain your release?

We shall mourn your loss until justice
is served.
We celebrate your courage,
your compassion.

We honor your memory
now and forever.

"The heaviest wheel rolls across
our foreheads
to bury itself deep somewhere
inside our memories.
We've suffered here more
than enough,
here in this clot of grief
and shame."

Lines from a poem written by Mif,
a child incarcerated in the Terezin
Concentration Camp, 1944

VERDI'S REQUIEM PLAYED AND SUNG BY JEWS IN TEREZIN CONCENTRATION CAMP
Summer--1944

First there is the embryo of an orchestra
and a small choir.
Instruments are brought into the ghetto.
Some of them are smuggled in
under loads of hay.
A battered piano is already there.
A double bass is spirited in by an SS man.
Everything finally comes together--
sheet music, instruments and a rehearsal room.
The work grows in stature with the large roster of
professional Jewish musicians.
For many days the musicians rehearse the score
under Rafael Schächter, the orchestra's
conductor.

How was the Camp Commandant able to set up
a concert hall for the presentation
of Verdi's Requiem?
It came into being through a military order
of the SS.
The order stated: "Evacuate the Jewish Hospital."
Sick Jews are evacuated,
loaded into carts and carriages.
The bodies of the dead are carried to the
crematorium.
In front of the hospital there is confusion
and uproar
mingled with the cries of the dying.
The sick are dumped in attics
with no water, lights, beds or blankets
in order to provide entertainment
for the SS and the Nazi brass.
The hospital is transformed into a theater.

Eichmann is impressed that the Jews

want to put on a performance of Verdi's Requiem
and that it will take place in a theater
with a full stage and gleaming footlights.
He tries to keep a straight face.
He doubles up with laughter
at the thought of the Jews ringing their own death knell
in the Requiem with its ancient Catholic prayers
about sin, damnation and hell.
But the Jewish prisoners know for whom the bell
really tolls.
They are alerted by reliable information from
outside sources.

Eichmann still wonders how the Requiem
with its Christian beliefs and motifs
can be played and sung by Jewish prisoners
in Terezin?
Don't the Jews know, he says, that in the Requiem
they'll be singing for themselves in hell?
Eichmann laughs again.
The kettle drums thunder
"The day of wrath has come!"
Orchestra, chorus and soloists unite
as one.
*"A final day will loose fire on the world
and leave it in ashes."*
The Jews already know the terror that shakes
each heart when God, the judge, sits
in judgment.
He will hold the Nazis accountable.
The *Tuba Mirum* rings loud and clear.
Verses flame in the abyss of fate
for men who enslave, rob, murder and
humiliate.

Eichmann listens, transfixed.

The basso profundo thunders across
the room
"Confutatis maledictis,"

the verse Mozart whispered as he lay
dying.
The choir sings with passion
"Libera me"
reaching out to life.

Instead of conducting the music
quietly as a solo
the conductor raises his baton and brings
it down fortissimo
with full orchestra, choir and kettle drums.
The room is crowded with Jewish prisoners
who are seated in front of Eichmann and
the SS.
Schächter tells his musicians in a final
rehearsal before the performance
to remember those who were tortured
and murdered by the Nazis.
Sing directly to the murderers, he tells them.

Schächter stands erect at the podium.
From the *Confutatis maledictis*
he moves to the *Recordata.*
A renowned Jewish opera singer,
a magnificent tenor, steps forward for his
grand aria.
"Groaning 'neath my sins,
I languish, Lord. Have mercy"
the singer prays.
He pleads and prays with desperate
groaning.

The music penetrates every heart
with stunning force.

"Confutatis maledictis"
the singers thunder.
The kettle drums roll.
The baton draws lightning from
the score.

"Lacrymosa!"
Schächter can barely contain himself.
Under his breath he cries out
Listen, you Nazi bastards,
you will not break us.
"Libera, Domine, de morte aeterna."

The choir is quiet. The soprano sings
"Tremens factus sum."
She repeats the words in a deep,
chilling recitative
as though an impartial judge were
pronouncing a death sentence
on the Nazis.
The cello joins in taking up the melody.
The conductor lets his baton fall
and raises his hand clenched into a fist.
He shouts the last words of the
Dies Irae.

Eichmann doesn't hear Schächter's
curses.
The conductor whispers to himself:
The day of wrath will come.
The German armies will be torn
to pieces.
Streams of blood will gush from
their wounds.
The whole world will witness the
downfall of Nazi Germany.
Justice will prevail.

The choir is singing fervently.
It stops singing.
The soprano's voice rings clear as
a great reverberating bell
"Libera me!"
Bells ring out in the orchestra.
Altos and tenors sing from all sides.

"Libera nos!
Libera nos!"
The huge choir thunders one last time.
The kettle drums boom--
three short strokes, one long.
Eichmann is visibly moved.
"Interesting. Very interesting"
he comments
as he applauds the musicians.

In early fall the train to Auschwitz stops
at the station in Terezin.
Schächter and his musicians are loaded
into the first cars of the first transport
to Auschwitz.

GHETTOS

AFTER GERMANY MADE HITLER ITS SAVIOR

The SS security guards, the elite of the
Nazi party
were recruited and trained to be cruel
and ruthless.
They wore the death's head-emblem
on their uniforms,
a skull and crossbones,
icon of intimidation and murder!
They conducted door to door searches
for Jews, Socialists, clergy,
Jehovah's Witnesses, trade union members,
homosexuals, unfriendly writers,
journalists, judges, lawyers, teachers
and foreigners.
A person could be arrested for any offense
or no offense at all.
The SS spied on the government
and on the SS itself,
looking for traitors and enemies.
The Jewish Book of Life and Death
lay open to the cyclonic fury
of the Holocaust
and the evil deeds of the Nazis
and their followers--
the lootings and shootings,
the gas chambers and crematoria.

Some victims fled, going into hiding,
desperate to get illegal documents
and fake identity cards,
In Lithuanian towns, Jews were hung
or burned in the streets.
Some arrived at the train stations
with broken arms and legs.
A rabbi from Wengrow was killed
on Yom Kippur.

He was ordered to sweep the street
and collect refuse in his hat.
When he bent over he was
bayonetted.

The Chelmno death camp,
near the city of Lodz, herded Jews,
eighty at a time in vans equipped
with gas.
Jews from seven ghettos in Greece
enroute to death camps in Poland
were packed so tightly in each
cattle car
they could not fall down, sleep
or defecate.
They stood for days.
Those who did not die enroute
were murdered on arrival.
The sound of gunfire
the sound of clubs pummeling
human flesh
mingled with the groans of the
dying.
The last *"Shema Yisrael"* of dying
Jews hovered in the air.
Before the clubs came down
they prayed for mercy
but the Germans paid no attention
to their pleas.

MOURNING

I sit *shiva* and begin to mourn today
for my family
in the mass graves of Poland
and in the flames of the Warsaw Ghetto.
They cry out to me
clutching me with their nails
that resemble hooks.
They want me to give them bones and flesh
a breath of life in my poetry
but what can I say to revoke their deaths?

In Biala Street. in Karmelicka Street
they were thrown on trucks, taken away
to be killed
all except my old, blind, crippled Aunt Malka
who was conveniently driven to the cemetery
and shot.
What can I say to my little cousin, Wlodek,
who also was taken, kicking and screaming
by Ghetto soul-snatchers wearing white
arm-bands?

NIGHT OF THE BROKEN GLASS
("Kristallnacht, Nov. 9, 1938")

My favorite doll has a china head.
Her head was smashed.

My mama cries until her eyes are red.

Tonight men with guns broke into our house.
They turned our furniture upside down.

They broke the chandelier and smashed
all the windows.

I was scared, scared,
I hid under my bed.

Mama begged them to stop.

They smashed everything in sight
even papa's violin

even mama's beautiful grand piano.
Every string was cut.

Down the street they burned our
synagogue.

The Torah scrolls shrieked and waved
their long arms.

Pain is frozen into the lines of mama's
face.

Papa says we must remember this night
and the bestiality of the Nazis.

He says we must escape from the Nazis
and emigrate to America.

Papa says our family has lived in Germany
for hundreds of years!

Papa is crying.

THE SHOAH
(Whirlwind-Holocaust)

Under an ominous sky trees uprooted themselves.
Dead branches whizzed by.

An old woman fell forward, blood dripping from
her forehead.

Great oaks bent down. They prayed like willows.
Their leaves streamed forward all in one direction.

Then everything fell on top of everything else.
The trees fell crown first.

The bark exploded. The trees screamed.
They split apart.

On the edge of town, trees fell on their knees
reciting the *Hineni.*

The wind blasted the trees.
It whipped, pounded, stripped them of leaves.

It trumpeted like a shofar:
Tekiah! Shevarim! Teruah! Tekiah!

Houses fell, mangled and twisted, under a sky
clenched like a blackened fist.

In a demolished synagogue a voice cried out
Ovinu Malkenu!

It was the voice of my mother praying for
redemption,
chanting the *Yaaleh* and the *Shema Kolenu!*

It was life rising in outbursts into meaning
stumbling over the roots of trees.

It was my mother on her knees chanting the last
Shema Yisrael of the dying.

RHAPSODY

Leaning over my piano I play
as though my life depended
on it.
Under each finger numb with
dread
people are running.
Some are shot dead.
Up against the platform
the cattle cars are waiting.
Fear in the eyes. Sweat.
A scream! A burst of fire!
My piano thrown from a window.
I continue to play.
For how many months, how many
years
the turning of axles
the grinding of gears?
I cannot stop the greedy engine
of death,
that relentless machine with
the bloody pistons.
It pounds away, pounds away.
I continue to play
in a world of ruins peopled by
phantoms.
Sobs rise from the sounding board.
Notes bleed under my fingers.
The keyboard and its keys
are coming unglued.
My days pass slowly like a candle
guttering out.
I hear the hooting of a train's hoarse
whistle
and the click-clacking of wheels
on the track
while in the distance a pile of ashes
where my relatives disappeared

is the place where I begin
my journey.

BLIND WALL

We are hiding behind a blind wall
as soldiers smash our dishes
tear down curtains, break our
furniture.
They are seizing the old.
They are nabbing little children
in raids on the Ghetto.
A baby starts crying.
Now we are lost.
We stuff his mouth with a pillow.
The mother cries.
The baby must be strangled.
Behind this wall we stand
like pillars of salt
still erect, having no place
to fall.

ATROCITIES

All night the moonlight leaks into my room.
I cannot sleep.
I toss in my bed.
The rabbi of Praga was beaten up.
In Plonsk, the weeping Jews were forced
to hack the holy Ark to pieces.
Small children crawl like rats through
the sewers.
Some soldiers threw an old man in his pajamas
out of the window,
flinging his pants after him.
A bureau drawer followed, even his bed.
The cobblestones are covered with blood,
with broken furniture and smashed window panes.
Rags and feathers settle over them.
Words fail me. I cannot speak.
My mouth stretches in a silent shriek:
"Abramele! Abramele!"

DANCING AND SINGING

The soldiers are making them take off their
clothes
and jump like frogs, goading them with
well-aimed blows.
An old, naked Jew leaps like a gazelle,
balances on one foot, scrapes and bows.
They are driving him mad with kicks
to the groin.
Hasidic Jews are ordered to dance naked around
a basket full of children's corpses.
They are forced to sing self-derogatory
songs.
An idle crowd laughs at their singing pitched
between a sob and a howl.
They watch the Hassidim driven with truncheons
and fists,
to the train station and from there to
Auschwitz.

IN THIS PASSOVER SEASON

They are staring and laughing
the butchers with medals
visiting the Ghetto as you would
a zoo
watching us die. Oh, the butchers!
May they strangle! May they choke!
May they give orders for the
last time.

Ma nishtanah ha leilah ha zeh
me kal ha lailos?
Why is this night different from all
other nights?
Because fists are banging on the door.
The table is overturned,
the plates broken, the wine spilled.
An egg is rolling across the floor.

They are wrecking furniture
and burning beds
breaking through walls.
The walls are shaking.
The plaster falls
on our world--a closet
with a false back.

LIKE SPARROWS SHIVERING

Jewish orphans huddle together
dying in the street
waiting for someone to take pity
on them.
They have no shoes.
Rags are wrapped around their feet.
Some are freezing to death
with almost no clothes and bare
feet.
They cry out at night.
Their cries haunt my sleep.

HEAR THIS

In our Polish village we were flogged by
the Germans
as we prayed in our synagogue
at the hour of sundown.
They tore the skullcaps from our heads.
They made us use our prayer shawls
as mops
to clean their latrines
while our captors bloodied us with clubs
and whips.
Helpless, we watched our synagogue burn.
We saw our rabbi beaten to death,
charged with praying to God for deliverance.
Two hundred of us were hanged and left
dangling out of our kitchen windows.
People were hanging on trees in the streets.
There were no streets without hanged men.
Some of us were hanging head downward.
Cut down, I lay in that hidden place
where emotions stay for years
without a trace
stuck in barbed wire.

THE DEATH PITS AT PONERY

On the night of Yom Kippur the Jews of the
ghetto
were herded through the streets of old Vilna,
a strange, eerie procession.
We held candles to light our way through
the blacked-out town.
Thousands of us were marched to our death
in Ponery
where nothing, not even light could escape.
As shots rang out we fell into a ravine.
When the murderers left I clawed my way out of
that bloody hell of cold, wet bodies.
A chorus of voices rose and fell sobbing
and choking.
Was it the sound of the wind feigning
sympathy?
Below me rose a mountain of corpses from
the death pits at Ponery.

MENORAH

It is Hanukkah in the Lodz Ghetto.
The arms of the *menorah* rise, disoriented.
Flames strain and twist.
The candles struggle with their short lives
just to exist.
The candles are a silent people.
They flicker out, flicker out
like the martyrs of the Lodz Ghetto
like prisoners riding the extended spur line
to death in Birkenau, Auschwitz-Birkenau
death in Dachau, Dachau-Kaufering
slaughtered in Vilna
murdered in Byalistok
liquidated in Lwow
executed in Volhymnia
massacred in Pinsk
eliminated in Lodz.
It is Hanukkah in the Lodz Ghetto.
Where are the Maccabees?

EFFORTS TO SAVE THE CHILDREN

Some Jewish parents gave their children
to Christian families
or to monasteries for safekeeping.
They did not know that some
of their children would be baptized
and raised as Christians.
Some Jews escaped the ghettos
in coffins
carried outside the ghetto
to the cemetery.
One family gave their child
a sleeping pill
and placed her in a coffin.
The father met the hearse at
the cemetery,
removed his child from the coffin
and fled with her.
Yizkor Elohim
May God remember
the sacrifices of these parents
for their children.

HOUSE OF DEATH

In the burning Ghetto a scream was thrown
out of a window
in a house walled and floored with agony.
Fires poured out of it.
The inhabitants of the house had no feet.
They were headless,
their eyes and mouths in their chests.
They spoke in telegrams.
They were dying of that horrible disease
called waiting, waiting for hunger and death
to overtake them.
They had no choice but to wait helplessly,
too old to fight with the Warsaw Ghetto
fighters.
They crouched, fetus-like,
in the emptiness of their lives,
blotting themselves into the darkness of
night
while the moon's eye peered like a laugh
in the wrong place
but I was there, mounting a staircase
of bent backs
descending on knotted blankets to death
and back
my eyes grafted on my heart.

ESCAPE THROUGH THE SEWERS

Many Jews who tried to escape death
by crawling through the sewers
of Warsaw
wandered around for many days
and nights
looking for a way out through
the narrow shafts of underground
tunnels.
Those of us who dared to risk the element
of chance
and the fetid waters, darkness, hunger
and agonizing thirst
crawled on our bellies,
slithered like snakes, crouched
half-upright
with lighted candles and guns,
a little water and a bit of bread,
moving slowly like turtles through
a maze of twists and turns
in an entombment out of world
and time.
Some died, some lived and made it
to the other side of Warsaw.
The prize: the lifting of a manhole cover
on the Aryan side--
sunlight and freedom.

Alerted to the presence of escaped
prisoners
the Germans blasted the manhole
with dynamite.
They shot bullets into it.
They pumped gas into it.
If you lost the game of chance
you died.
If you won you're still alive.
Some died, some lived.
The Germans left the area assuming

all of us were dead.
Fiction pales before the filth
and horror of the sewers.
Some of us emerged half-alive
and made our way to the forests,
our lives still torn apart in turmoil.
We played survival roulette
and won.

UPRISING IN THE WARSAW GHETTO

Week after week there are unclaimed bodies
rotting in the streets.
Men are weeping for their wives and children
but the dead stay dead in this godforsaken
kingdom.
Pinkert, king of the dead, loads his pushcart
with bodies.
Bodies are thrown from one streetcar to the
next
until somebody claims them.
Too much, too much for Jews to live dying.
They will strike a blow for freedom.
What meaning is there in slow starvation
while the full breast of the moon hangs
pendulous and dripping from the branches
of a tree?

CONTEMPT FOR DEATH

On the eve of Passover in the year '43
the Freedom Fighters of the Warsaw Ghetto
united to fight.
On Day One of the Uprising the Germans
came marching into the Ghetto,
marching in columns, ready to attack.
Jewish fighters hid everywhere
ready to fight back.
They waited on blind corners
in cellars and attics.
As the Germans approached Jews pelted them
with Molotov cocktails and hand grenades.
They took deadly aim.
Their one machine gun mowed down the Nazis.
The attackers suffered such a devastating
blow
they fled in terror.
Jewish fighters twice forced a retreat.
Then the Germans brought a tank into the
Ghetto.
A quiet, well-aimed throw of a bottle
hit the tank.
It went up in flames.
Freedom fighters pursued the Germans
from house to house.
Their bullet-riddled flags fluttered proudly.
With contempt for death the Jews
fought on.

WOMEN OF VALOR

Women who resisted the Ghetto slaughter:
Frume, Fagel, Tamar, Liba
moving over rooftops hurling grenades
at the Nazis below
you are messengers of hope
human links from ghetto to ghetto,
you stand tall like Sarah, Rachel
and Rebecca.

Halinka, daughter of a Hassidic father,
you refused to leave when your family escaped.
You said you no longer belonged to yourself
but to your comrades in the Resistance.
At the height of a fierce battle
you saw a gun pointed at your Commander.
Without hesitation you shielded her
with your own body.
You were killed by the bullet meant for her.

Women of valor, your worth is far above
rubies.
You accepted each day a frightening tiding
of Job.
You aided and comforted the wounded--
You, Regina, who searched for combat squads
declaring your intention of returning
through the sewers
to bring back stranded fighters.
The sewers were flooded.

You who died in a hail of bullets
buried in wrecked bunkers
killed in shoot-outs,
I shall remember you and honor
your memory
by hurling myself against oppression
never yielding to the dark god
of tyranny and hatred.

THERE SHALL BE TIME NO LONGER

German tanks lumber into the Ghetto
like monsters of the Apocalypse.
Planes drop poison gas.
The Germans bomb the hospital where
Jews lie sick.
In the undestroyed halls they massacre
patients.
In the delivery room they bayonet
the bellies of women in childbirth.
They raze the Ghetto.
They fill the underground sewer-routes
with water,
They blow up the exits laying siege to
bunkers.
The Ghetto is a wasteland shrouded in
silence
Lost lives are like pieces of ancient
pottery buried in a city
whose inhabitants are ghosts.

Who are these men who pop out of
the charred ground
faces unshaven, clothing tattered,
weapons in hand?
Wild-looking women with matted hair
emerge from the ruins
children resembling forest creatures
crawl out in search of water.

DEPORTATIONS

A WHEEL OF FORTUNE WITH RAZOR-SHARP KNIVES

A wheel of fortune with razor-sharp knives points to
men targeted for death

while a church choir in black robes sings baroque music
from the seventeenth century.

A locomotive draws its interminable length along the horizon.

It is moving a human cargo to places of torture.
The dead multiply.

The wheel of fortune turns again and again.
Knives leap out stabbing.

Handel's *Messiah* fills the soot-filled air.

NIGHT JOURNEY TO POLAND

I hear the heavy, rhythmical panting,
the fearful hissing of a coal locomotive
idling in the station.
I hear the *geshrei* of the engine's
whistle
as the train pulls out of the Umschlagplatz
pulling a line of cattle cars.
The way is strange and dislocated.
Mysterious fires are burning.
The moon hangs fire casting evil
shadows.
Clouds glow all night.
The thick, biting smoke is real.
The ashes are real.
The smell of death hangs over Poland.
A wounded songbird flies into
the forest
and does not return.

HOLOCAUST

Every day I try to banish my fright, yet I dream
the same dream night after night:
The train to Auschwitz is loaded with corpses.
My fingers are tongue-tied trying to pass on
this secret message to an amputated hand.
The rain is falling in bloody gobbets.
The sun explodes from the barrel of a gun.
From the end of a rope the last hope dwindles.
Stalled in the very middle of nowhere.
Return--where? From what? To what?
Gaffed like a fish with its throat torn out
my body stiffens curved and bent double.

Tombstones are toppled and graves are dug up.
In a ravine in Poland men are digging up thousands
of corpses
with open mouths and projecting tongues--
Jews buried alive
engulfed by firing squads, devoured by flames,
choking for breath in gas-filled chambers.

The sun is setting and the valley is filled with
shadows.
Trees stand black and flat against the sky
crying out like Old Testament prophets
while an orchestra of birds sings making a lyrical
racket in the branches.
Horrors multiply.
Fields painted with wildflowers spring up around me.
I cannot return to a picture-perfect day.
A clock ticks the hours away.
The wind carries the smell of decaying bodies.
The people of Lublin close their windows.

THE CHILDREN MUST BE DEPORTED

An anti-Jewish poster in France in 1941 declared openly: "Jews must be swept away to make our house clean."

The children must be deported.
If we don't deport them
the French police and the Vichy regime
will have to be involved in their long-term
care.
Feeding and educating them will be
the sole responsibility of the government.

It is absolutely necessary to deport
the children
before problems are created that will
last for years
for if the Germans are defeated
and the children grow up
they will want to know what happened
to their parents
and will demand an accounting
from those responsible for their
deaths.

The children must be deported.
Without them the number of deportees
will fall short of the numbers
needed to fill the quota.
When the mothers weep
and plead with you to let them
keep the children--
beat them back with your rifle butts.

THE CHILDREN MUST NOT BE FORGOTTEN

A piercing wail comes from a railcar
standing on a side track.
The multi-voiced wailing continues
unabated
in the boxcar full of small frightened
children.
Their shaven heads can be seen in
the barred window.
Three year olds and some barely two
sob for their mothers.
11,400 Jewish children were arrested
in France
and deported to concentration camps
where they were gassed and their
bodies burned.

How could the French police cooperate
with the Nazis
by wrenching small children from
their mothers' arms?
How could they put the little ones
in sealed boxcars?
A small boy, eight years old,
throws himself on his baby sister,
takes her in his arms and cries out,
"Don't take her away from me.
She's all I have left."

FATHER OF ORPHANED CHILDREN

The children of the Ghetto beg for food,
ragged creatures, little starvelings.
One child clutches a gray rag doll
with lolling head and limp body.
Here comes Korczak,[1]
"Father of orphaned children."
He gives them bread
and accompanies them on the train
to Treblinka.
He will not abandon his young
charges
even to save his own life.
Offered safe passage out of Poland
he refuses to let the children
travel alone on the death train, yes,
even to save his own life
he will not abandon the children.
They die together.

JEWS, STEP FORWARD

You climb into the wagon of the first
transport
moving quietly with averted eyes,
let out at the gas chamber disguised
as a shower room.
Only now do you understand
what it is all about
the meaning of the shouts
the whistles of command
"Bewegung! Bewegung!"
The SS guards are working hard
working overtime to kill, kill, kill.
"Jews, enter the shower room."
"Walk quickly to the edge of
the trench."
Here, you will know the dead by
the stench of blood stiffening
in pools of red
and the smell of flesh broiling
as the Jews in the crematorium
float up to heaven.

MASSACRE

Weeping, the Kapo loads his mother
into the cattle car.
The deportees stand pressed together.
The train moves on.
A time to live and a time to die.
Resettlement in the East--
the age-old question: Why? Why?
In Kolomai
in Kamenetz-Podolsk
in Babi Yar
women killed on shore
men pushed into the sea.
The very old, the crippled, shot
on the spot.
The train moves forward with
a cry for help
from the engine's screaming
whistle.

ARRIVALS AND DEPARTURES

Squeezed out of every corner of Europe
Jews are herded into boxcars sealed shut.
Who is arriving? Who is departing?
All day the chimneys cough up ashes
and smoke.
Whose flesh is burning?
Whose body is feeding the ovens?

The tears of all the rivers on earth
poured into one vast fire extinguisher
cannot put out the fires.
Death waits for us.
We wait in the snow.
We wait in the rain.
Our bodies slump.
In what language shall we cry out?

CONFLAGRATION

I am locked in a cattle car crowded with
Jews.
I, too, am a prisoner on my way to death
suffocating in the smoke of hysteria
women shrieking, children crying
old men dying, their heads bowed--
an exodus of people in a never-ending
nightmare.
The days pass in pain and fear.
I lose my head
I lose the thread of my life
I lose all the threads of my identity.
Death says, *"Komm."*
I reply, *"Ich?"*
Death answers,
"Ja, du."
With the words of the *"Shema"*
on my trembling lips
I enter the flames
with the souls of all the Hasidim
dancing.

THE LAST WORDS SPOKEN

Let me begin with the
last words spoken
how I prayed
we would be strong
enough to resist
the hands of death
ready to bury us.
In the night we carried
babies and bundles
through a sea of
frightened faces heads
flying off minds
bending out of shape
walking a tightrope
of fear sliding
falling with our babies
in our arms
trees gliding
stones thudding
feet stumbling
caught like a ram
in a thicket walking
in darkness walking
in darkness
walking

THE DEATH CAMPS

IN THE WORLD OF SUFFERING AND DEATH

The sound of thunder from gunfire
echoes from the hills.
From whence cometh our help?[1]
The last *Shema Yisrael* pierces
the air.
Ani ma' amin rises in silence
from the lips of old men,
their faces averted.
"I believe in the coming of the Messiah.
Though He may tarry, yet will He come.
As for man, his days are as grass; as
a flower of the field, so does he bloom.
A wind passes and the flower is gone
and its place never sees it again."[1]
The windows of our bodies are broken.
"Night racks our bones."[2]
All the doors to the future lie
unhinged.

THE EXCAVATOR

The engine of the excavator rumbles
and pants
clawing graves out of the sand
plunging its steel arm into the sand
digging with its hand
waiting for prisoners to fall dead
in the sand
the cold yellow sand.
Oh! The constant grinding of metal
on sand
Oh! The excavator!
May it smash its hand on immovable
rocks
May it fall apart
May it be devoured by quicksand!

DEATH JEW

You keep running. You throw at top speed.
If you stop you are dead.
Running means life.
The grave site is new.
You load a Jew on your empty stretcher
sometimes two to avoid the bullet
aimed at you.
At night one suicide follows another.
When you hear the cry, "Away!"
you know someone has hung himself.
You help him die.
You removed the box under his feet.
You try to sleep.
In the morning you keep running
throwing at top speed.
Running means life.
If you stop you are dead.

STONES, COLLECT STONES

"**Y**ou need no luggage. You need no watches.
Money is useless here.
Writing is forbidden so hand over your pens.
Stones, collect stones!"
We lift heavy rocks by day
and throw them in again at night.
I sleep as though a stone were under my head.
A stone falls into my dreams.
I swallow it with one great gulp.
I am covered with stones, large and small.
Who can swallow them all?
In one corner of a field stand a wall
of stones.
They fall down.
They crawl over each other.
They break into a run.
"Stehenbleiben!" Stop! Stop!

MAUTHAUSEN

A fusillade of curses, then shots ring out,
then silence.
Anguished faces of prisoners emerge,
their heads shaved, bodies, chalk-white.
The guards have no remorse,
no feelings of shame or regret for
condemning Jewish prisoners to horrific
suffering and death.
In Mauthausen no birds build nests.
No trees or flowers grow in this lifeless
landscape.
Rocks huddle under a scowling sky.

The camp specializes in working prisoners
to death in the rock quarry.
120,000 out of 200,000 men, women
and children die of neglect,
overwork, sadistic torture and murder
through starvation and beatings.
Prisoners are forced to run up 189 steps
from the camp's granite quarry
carrying stones weighing over 100 pounds.
If the stones are dropped, they crush
the feet of those behind them.

Every Jew who drops his load is beaten
mercilessly
and the stone is again lifted to his
shoulders.
In despair, many commit suicide by leaping
into the quarry from the cliff above.
Some are thrown over the edge by guards.
Prisoners are murdered by being forced
to run into electrified fences
or are shot in the back of the neck
or killed with chemicals injected directly
into the heart

Mauthausen is like a photograph of evil
incarnate
acted out in multiple exposure by
deeply disturbed men.
Guards give orders and shout irrational
commands
motivated by paranoia, systematized
delusions
and the Nazi fantasy of male omnipotence
making the Jews
contemptible objects to be dominated
and worked to death.

EVERYTHING LEADS TO THE STOVES

The fields are covered with cabbages
fertilized with human ashes.
In one corner lie charred, half-burned
skeletons.
First the gas chambers, then the stoves.
Life is a failed, tragic vaudeville act.
The dead are dragged away with hooks.
Starving prisoners toil at the stoves.
In a month, they, too, will go into
the stoves.
All paths lead to the stoves.
Little children are taken alive to the
stoves.
They are undressed, shot and thrown
into the stoves.
The stoves receive them without guilt
or remorse.

THEY FOUGHT BACK

In the cellar rooms of the crematorium at
Heydebreck
the prisoners fought their guards.
The guards counterattacked
with flames-throwers and guns.
They killed the prisoners who crossed
the threshold.
The remaining prisoners were marched to
the gas chamber.
Proudly they sang *"Hatikvah"*.
Defiantly they sang the Czech National
Anthem.

IN THE SHADOW OF THE HOLOCAUST

REMEMBERING BELLS RINGING IN KISHINEV
(Pogrom--April 6, 1903)

Why were the church bells ringing in Kishinev?
Ringing wildly at noon?
Bells going berserk.
Bells on a rampage--
Bells ringing ferociously on the last day
of Passover?
Mobs in the streets shouted
"Kill the Jews!"
They rushed about with axes and clubs.
They rioted, they killed,
never getting their fill.
The city officials refused to intervene.
They remained in their houses
behind windows and screens,
cold in their knowing eyes
cold in their knowing eyes.

HIS HANDS WEPT

His hands wept as he waited for her on every corner.
His hands wept among the ruins of dead streets.

His hands wept huddled together out in the open.
His hands wept for the speech of the unspoken.

His hands wept for the charred skull in the Dachau
ovens.

His hands wept as he dreamed of nights
in the garden of love and desire

His hands wept as one incomparable hand
touched the other

His hands wept for leave-taking understood
without good-bye.

THE SILENT ONES

I see those who died yesterday
and the day before yesterday
and the day before the day before yesterday
a whole people dying.
At last I stop asking why
the murderer murders
why bombs drop and houses go up in flames
why children are caught and carried away
screaming
why in beautiful synagogues windows crash
why wars destroy without pity
and without pause
why no one is accountable to the dead
for the onlookers are also perpetrators.

WHAT IS IT ALL ABOUT?

Monday arrives dragging a big sack of letters.
No letter from you.

A slow old freight rumbles in the distance.
The train is late.

I hear doomed cattle bawling in their boxcars.

I see Jews dying in crowded boxcars,
the old, the sick, the crippled, the orphans.

I see the Torah and old prayer books
set on fire in a synagogue.

I see the four letter name of God holding
all the powers of eternity.

I think of the bread of affliction--
the unleavened bread baking on the rocks.

I see a drizzle of ash raining down,
struggling for definition.

WHO WAS ANNA WACHALSKA?

Who was Anna Wachalska who lived
in Warsaw
at the time of the German invasion
and helped Jewish Resistance Fighters
escape to the forest?
Who was this brave woman?
Was she murdered or imprisoned
by the Nazis?
Did she live to old age
with loving husband, children and
grandchildren beside her?
What happened to her?
I don't even know if Anna Wachalska
is her real name.
Did she remain a Polish freedom
fighter--
this woman who lived out the principles
of honor and human dignity,
who fought for the liberation of
Poland from Germany?
She heard the knocking at the gate
of her heart
and gave the identity of her own
dead daughter
to a young Jewish woman.

THE SURVIVORS

We who outlived the transports and camps
We who survived the pits overflowing
with lifeless bodies
We who outlived the ghetto's rebellion
the fight for freedom doomed to defeat by
huge Nazi forces, their machine guns
their tanks
as they set the whole ghetto on fire
We who lived and escaped to tell the story
We who are commanded in our hearts
to survive as Jews
We who are commanded in our hearts
to die as Jews
We who are exhorted to remember
in our bones
the martyrs of the Holocaust
so they shall not have died in vain
We who outlived the corpses hanging
on the fences, drying like laundry
We who drank soup tasting of corpses
We who are proud to cry out like the prophet
Jonah
"Ivri anochi! I am a Hebrew"--
must save the children of the world
dying in the flames of hate
for the evils of the world are as Dachau
and Auschwitz
but we who have learned nothing
and forgotten everything
are commanded to stand in our graves
and recite the *Kaddish* for ourselves,
for ourselves!

TRIUMPH OF THE DEAD

Purple smoke no longer belches from the smokestacks
of the crematoria.
The night sky is no longer red.
The smell of putrefaction no longer fills the air.
Prisoners who collapsed no longer lie where they fall
or are thrown on carts and removed to a pyramid
of still-breathing corpses.
German prisoners are ordered to "Spread it.
Spread it!"
Instead of guns they carry rakes.
They spread the ashes of Jewish prisoners
over the field.
High brick chimneys are beaten to the ground
with sledge hammers.
Signs above the showers are smashed with axes.
The electric current flowing through triple rows of
barbed wire no longer flows.
Signs that lied to newly arrived prisoners
declaring "Work will make you free"
are ripped down and burned on the spot.
For the Nazis the world is fraught with incoherence
as scratchings and clawings become a tumult
of sound
rising from the ashes.

A VISIT TO AUSCHWITZ

Ashes, tons of ashes, are preserved
in a huge monument
so the wind can't scatter them.
Many tourists visit the gas chambers
and ovens
that were part of *die Entlösung*--
the catastrophe that overtook Europe
and turned burnt offerings of
human beings
into thousands of pounds of ashes.

Visitors say memorial prayers in Auschwitz
and place lighted candles in the ovens
to remember the souls of all who
were gassed
whose bodies were burned to hide
the evidence of their deaths.
Preserved in dark torments
their trembling voices cry out.

JEW DOLLS

Craftsmen in Poland carve wooden Jews
for the tourist trade.
Christians buy them as amulets
to ward off evil.
They symbolize for the Polish people
healing and reconciliation with
Poland's Jews.
Jews buy the Jew-dolls with their
tiny skullcaps and twisted sideburns
as a poignant reminder of those
who died in the Holocaust.

The Polish woman behind the counter
in the gift shop outside Auschwitz
wraps up a Jew-doll.
for an American visitor touring
the extermination camp.
"He has an old soul," she says.
"He hears the things you are thinking.
Take him with you to America.
He will grow on you."

SONG OF THE RETURN

Who can fail to sense the glory in the reality of a people restored, of a people regaining its dignity, after having been defamed and marked for destruction? In anticipation of the return to the Land the psalmist sings:

> *"When the Lord brought the exiles back to Zion*
> *we were like those who dream. "*
>   Psalm 126: 1

The power of promise, the power of hope...necessitated the resurrection of Israel...the wonder of the risen Israel...martyred Israel raised from the dead. We are witnesses of the resurrection. And being a witness is transformation. There is the possibility of redemption for all men. Stand still and behold! The unbelievable has come about. The return to the Land. It is like the ladder of Jacob pointing to Jerusalem on high. The mystery that is Jerusalem, the challenge that is Jerusalem!
                    Abraham Joshua Heschel

ASCENT

In mythological Jerusalem the air itself
is all-illuminating.
The evergreen trees stand tall and proud
their tops in brightness.
All around hands join with each other
creating a world of their own
reconciling opposing pulls
and allowing the mystery of Jerusalem
to remain intact.
Some day I shall visit Jerusalem
with hymns of praise
and the beating of kettle drums.
With the gift of my words
I shall visit Israel without announcing
myself
by word or deed.
On a day lighter than crystal I shall come
softly with quiet steps.
And a fine bright joy shall pour through
my body
and a stone fall from my breast.

UNITING DREAM AND REALITY IN ISRAEL

You yearn to visit Israel, not just to be
there in your thoughts and imagination.
Suppose Isaac the Blind[1] were to
accompany you to Safed?
What if Yedidiah[2] urged you to
unite dream and reality and to
experience for yourself the historical,
metaphysical weight of millennia
in that land?
We are all part of the mystical
body of Israel--
those who are Jews by birth
those who are Jews by choice
and those who identify with
the Jewish people
and the birth of Israel,
a sliver of land far away--
enduringly hopeful.

ISRAEL OF ALL GENERATIONS

Suppose time, questioning you, follows
you everywhere, do not turn around.
Suppose it stares and stares at you
do not turn around.
A voice in your dream recites these
words:
You must go up the steps
and down the steps of your life
in the here-and-now
but you long to fly to Israel instead
and tour the land and spend
time in Jerusalem, Tel Aviv, the seaport
of Haifa
and the ancient city of Safed.
With all your heart you want to go
there.
Time and distance that held you back
will no longer hold you back.
The eyes of all the Jewish martyrs
are upon you.

Israel is a symphony in the shape of
words, in the form of deeds.
And the mystery that is Jerusalem
is a recalling, a believing
and the undying hope that the Jewish
people will continue to live
in their own country, their ancient
homeland.
I shall not forget you, beloved
Jerusalem!
While the brightness of the sun washes
space, light rinsed and glowing,
I am flying over Israel inch by inch
from a height of millennia
ready to land on the runway.

INTOXICATIONS OF DIVINITY

Jerusalem! Your name, blessed, washes over me
like an eternal Amen
lapping how many wars, how many griefs,
how many deaths?
O, my Jerusalem! You have triumphed in a way
no one could have foreseen.
The sight of your walls softly honeyed with
light
moves me to tears,
you, so exalted in faith that in your streets
love walks without footprints.

The inborn shining of your forehead shimmers
like the dazzling glare of a sun on water
shining with infinite grains of memory
never to forget, never to forget
intoxications of divinity! Conversations--
I-and-Thou
between the desert and the sown.
You rise above worlds hurled from their
pedestals,
poised in your gemlike setting like a great
carved opal.

How I yearn for you, my Jerusalem!
Your sharp-sided hills, your light-filled sky
cry me to return.
Oh, Jerusalem, I am greedy for your
caresses.
I cannot bear my days and nights
without you,
the tight embrace by which you hold me
after starving night.
How shall I describe my love for you
with eyes brimming over with
tears of joy.

THE SONG OF THE RETURN

We wandered in the desert of the Diaspora
lost and in a daze for generations.

Some of us had faith in our hearts, others,
despair.

Some of us sang a song of hope and redemption,
others, a song of immolation.

Like the Altar Flame spirited away to a secret
hiding place

some of us bore the seed of the future within
ourselves.

Others, like Samson, brought down the pillars
of Faith.

Some of us remained rooted in the Jewish tradition.

Others wandered like homeless spirits in the heat
of the afternoon.

Some of us died in the Spanish Inquisition
and walked among the ruins of Kishinev.

Some of us set our sign and seal upon our people
in the fiery conflagration of the Holocaust.

Others cherished their own small candle flames
and were lost.

The onslaught against us, like a ponderous mountain
of water, rose in wild fury
and crashed down on us.

God Himself was faint from the terrifying thunder
that issued from His own mouth.

In this world in which Cain is still killing
Abel

we descended into the grave, a Congregation of
the Dead,

and came up alive with the Torah in our arms
to fulfill the Promise of the Return

planted in Israel never again to be plucked up.

PSALM OF HOPE

Sound the great horn for freedom!
Gather the exiles from all corners of
the earth.
Let them not vanish from history
or die like Samson who, having fought
against the Philistines.
was betrayed, captured and blinded.
Let multitudes sing in the Valley
of the Bones.

In the crowded alleys of Old Jerusalem
the houses turn inward.
A black mist of blood still clings to
the site
where David wrested Jerusalem from
the Jebusites
and made its hills his beloved city.
Even from the beginning it was a sacred
place.
Rise up, O six million, from the Valley
of Shadow.
Stand, Job, in the dust and ashes of
your faith.

The lopping waves knock louder and louder
on Israel's shore
engulfing the land with stinging showers.
Who fed you on quails and manna
in the desert?
He shall feed you again in the wilderness.
Dry river beds shall turn into torrents
following cloud by day and fire by night.
O, sing again from the heights of Zion.

HOPE AND REDEMPTION

If you listen you will know
the hour has struck
to sing for land and people
to sing for this Remnant
living in Israel.
I lift my voice to my people
Their spirit is poured
into my poetry
sweetening every sorrow
healing every pain.
Fruit and sap, root and foliage,
I love this land
where love is a *mitzvah*
a divine command.

Singing and shouting come the
descendants of the prophets.
They speak the Hebrew language
ancient and profound.
Beyond the silence of the sphinxes
and pyramids
they guard the miracle of their
lives reclaimed.
Beyond the ruins of Assyria
the wasteland of Babylonia
I listen for the echo of
forgotten generations.
I walk across vast stretches of
time.
The call of blood will not be
silenced.

Some day I'll visit Jerusalem again,
in memory of my grandmother
who wanted to be buried there
on the Mount of Olives.
I shall bow my head against the Wall
until my eyes overflow with tears.

I shall roll myself in the dust
of Israel.
I shall sing the song of hope and
redemption, of human freedom.
I shall journey to Israel
across thousands of miles
weeping and laughing
to hold in my hand the sunlit stones
of the Promised Land.

EVER-PRESENT IN MY LIFE

Israel is a book in which past history
is present
in which the present is inconceivable
without millennia gone by
a modern-day book with an ancient
aura
that continues to be written,
sanctified by the suffering of a whole
people
a people devoured by a word
as the prophets were devoured.
Many a martyrdom was for a scroll.
God came and gave Ezekiel
a scroll
and He said, "Eat the scroll.
Don't read it, eat it."

Holy land of our forefathers
and foremothers
the past is prologue, the future
shimmers with hope.
Remember, God, the words of
your prophets:
"The stone shall cry from the wall
and the beam in the woodwork shall
echo the call."[1]
Here gathered together are your
scattered people
from the four corners of the world:
"I will plant them upon their land
and they shall never again
be uprooted."[2]

TRANSFORMATIONS

Nothing is lost in the world, not even the vapor
that issues from our mouths. Like everything
else, it has its place and its destination.
Nothing falls into a void for all things have
their place.

from the *Zohar*

TRANSFORMATIONS

A SHARE IN THE WORLD TO COME

In the year '81 turned incandescent
I became a parable, my life a myth.
Transfigured by the will to persist
my words were vehement, volatile,
singling me out for a new beginning
fed by the fires of *kiddush hashem*.
Words inscribed in the Book of Life,
words transcending the limits of
believing,
hanging gardens of words
words from the *neshamah*[1]
words making the angels into winds[2]
words wearing the phylacteries of
the head and arm
words set as a seal upon the heart
words with a share in the world
to come.
O may my words "like the bones of
the pious, wherever they are interred,
keep rolling underground to Jerusalem."

TRANSFORMATIONS

A long time ago there was an old woman
whose hormones were still raging.
She searched in the holy books
for the meaning of her remaining years.
She saw that life was a series of deaths
and resurrections, sometimes sad,
sometimes tragic, sometimes beautiful.
She knew she had little time left
to experience the thrills of passionate excess
and the exhilaration of creation *ex nihilo*
for she was eighty-three years old.

She saw that deep down, much lower than
Everest is high
a black-crowned night heron was still
flying over mysterious ground
while an angel with dizzy blue hair
flirted with the world of the innermost soul
in the presence of the angel of death
full of eyes from head to foot.
She saw a ladder with rungs endlessly
climbing up and down.
She experienced life's changeable moods
in a world where the real and the imagined
are inseparable.
She saw a *minyan* of pine trees swaying
back and forth in prayer.
Her illuminated thoughts reached critical
mass.
Her energy turned time and space
inside out
in the flow of lines and strange shapes
as order and proportion vanished
in a torrential downpour.
For an instant she was like Elijah who
ascended to heaven on the wings
of a tempest.

The old woman understood she would
appear ridiculous and foolhardy
to other people
for she had to fling herself over a cliff
in order to transform herself.
Some people called her Preposterella--
the-one-who-is-expendable.
Others called her Vesselina--
recipient of Platonic essences.
Still others called her Extravaganza,
bejeweled with loose hair flowing,
riding on the strong hips of God.

In her last incarnation she was honored
in the Book of Splendor
as the Splendiferous One who brought
brightness and joy to the Land
while bells rang out compellingly
harmonious,
all resonating with one another
in gardens within a garden
in the land where Will holds the balance,
Mercy expands and Justice prevails.
Yet the vision still awaits its time.
"If it be slow, wait for it; it will surely
come."[1]

I FOUND THE KEY TO A HOLY PLACE

I found the key to a holy place
by winding my way back
to the start of things.
I made marks on paper
overflowing with meanings
illuminating the alphabet
of love.
Thoughts and feelings kept
remaking themselves
like a kaleidoscope with
its shifting patterns.

The personalities of the letters
merged in the sharing of
extravagant gestures
yet each was separate
in its restraint.
They exchanged savors and essences
filling the air
with the pungent aroma of cinnamon,
vanilla, cardamom and clove.

They developed fabled themes,
then returned to them
and played them out in different ways
with all the resources of
metaphorical language
from a memory so ancient,
so introspective,
I have lost the name for it.

The words arranged themselves,
seeming effortless
and seemingly produced from
almost nothing.
I worked without a blueprint
under chairs, in corners,
in drawers, in a bookcase--

in that space where mystery
does not wish to be known.

Because so many words are
easily frightened
and can live in the present
only as transients,
I threw *this* together with *that*
and came up with something else,
turning my life into poetry
and my poetry into life
so that I might arrive
where I was already.

ON THE DAY OF ATONEMENT

I dreamed my father and his father
stood before me
in medieval black clothes.
The dried leaves of their prayer books
opened to places only the devout
can penetrate.
The mystical letters flew out, alive
with desire
and the holiness of the heart's
affections
boldly etched in black fire on white fire.
The letters lifted themselves up
in laughter and song,
then returned to the prayer books.

In faraway Uzda, my grandfather placed
his trembling hands on my head
and blessed me with his love.
He told me to be, not like the ceiling,
out of reach,
but like the threshold that enters
into a new life.
He said words are the love letters
of God
that I read but do not understand
and that what I say and how I say it
proclaim who I am
and that where my thoughts are,
there I am.

Then my dead father spoke to me
in the sanctuary of B'nai Jeshurun.
He said: Remember the words of
the Bratzlaver Rebbe.
One who is able to write a book
and does not do it
is as one who has lost a child.
It is also written in the *Zohar*

Nothing drops into a void,
neither words nor the voice of
a person.

I wept knowing my lips were
sealed shut with a burning coal.
What could I say as my voice struggled
to find its register,
my syllables to free themselves,
the words to stop strangling
in my throat.
What work of atonement was God asking
me to do
for the sin of being thrown off course
for the sin of being tempted and misled
for the sin I committed with utterance
of the lips
for the sin I committed by being stiff-necked
for the sin I committed with confusion
of mind
and the sin I committed in presumption
or error.

My father answered me by chanting
the *Kol Nidrei* on an ever higher note.
Then God answered me:
Keep fanning the holy sparks
and keep feeding the fire.
Go out from your tribulations
from darkest night into eternal sunlight
and facing Jerusalem
take three steps backward
and three steps forward
reciting the *Amidah*
then write the book you were meant
to write.
It is your destiny to write
as you wrestle with your dark angel.

I TURNED THE PAGES OF A BOOK ON THE LIFE OF A POET

I turned the pages of a book on the life of a poet
written in invisible ink on her flayed skin.
The book was covered with dust from a lifetime of
confronting questions of visceral impact
as old memories were set to rest
and new ones were set in motion in radiant
voice
exultant one moment
elegiac the next
while destruction hovered over every thought
in mythopoetic, uprushing sentences
in her search for her own voice
and identity.

In a mood of exaltation I slipped inside
the paperback tractate of the poet's life with
its inner imperatives.
Was her work a theme and variations?
A tone poem? A concerto?
Or was it orchestral music that could be
heard faintly in the top row of the balcony?
Was her work like lightning streaking across
the sky
igniting fears and tensions
or was it like Icarus's impossible dream of
transcendence?

Her life passed through a mountainous
landscape
through rivers and oceans
before plunging over cliffs to the breakers
below.
Her tears withheld wore boulders away
and carved mountains into canyons.
Flood waters lifted above her head.
She lifted her arms in a circular motion

in an effort to contain the forming
and melting
the tightening and loosening
appearing and disappearing
giving and withholding
creating and concealing

the hastening and delaying
flowering and decaying
softening and congealing
caressing and bruising
subsiding and cresting like bells
in a bell tower ringing
the melody of her life entwining
limbs and emotions
ringing out in harmonic modulations
and transformations
in chordal outbursts
in music that rushes at the listener
as if from nowhere
while flocks of birds act like
guardian angels--
a testament to the restorative power
of faith and love.

A SOUL ON FIRE

On Rosh Hashanah
on the very first day of new Beginnings
the day of the Turning--
The Book of the Tortured and the Slaughtered
opens before Him.
The body returns to ashes
but the soul is transformed into a deep
knowing that gives birth to light
in a cosmic quickening
a divine fire
while the roots of the Days of Awe
continue to grow.

THE JOURNEY UPWARD AND INWARD

I can climb the sacred ladder of halls
from hall into hall into hall into hall--
the greater halls and the lesser halls
squeezed together like the kernels of
nutshells one within the other--
or I can return to the first rung of the ladder
and keep my foot on the first step.
It bears the full brunt of winds and storms.
Instead I climb toward the Source
holding fast to the letters of the alphabet.
There are still many mornings left
to stir up holy communion
accompanied by song.

HOPE AND REDEMPTION

BEGIN THIS DAY

Begin this day with infinity and eternity.
Read a portion of the Pentateuch.
Welcome the ultimate Sabbath
but end with a question instead of an answer.
Answers keep changing.
Only the questions are eternal.
Begin the Torah while standing on one foot.
Sha! Be quiet and let the prow of your little boat
take you forward and forward forever.
Let the unicorn dip his aphrodisiac horn
into the persistence of your vision.
Be a pivot instead of a pawn.
In the half-light in which enigmas flourish
cherish, understand and protect the enigma.
It is not for nothing that you hear a clock ticking
where there is no clock, a distant bell,
a phrase of music seducing you.
It is not for nothing that the Word continually
shapes your life, that you wrestle with it
like a mighty Jacob with his demons,
like Ruth who followed her mother-in-law
to her own land.
Begin, perceive and understand why distant
galaxies are at your door.

SHOFAR BLOWER

He holds the ram's horn curved side up.
He grasps it in his right hand.
When the caller calls out *"Tekiah"*
he blows the sound of *Tekiah*.
When the caller calls *"Shevarim Teruah"*
he blows *Shevarim Teruah*.
When the caller calls *"Tekiah"* again,
he blows *Tekiah*.
He responds to the caller three times.
Then the caller calls out *"TEKIAH GEDOLAH!"*
The ram's horn blower makes the last note
of the shofar last as long as there is
breath in his body--
He holds it, seemingly forever,
His face lights up like a great torch.
Tekiah Ge-do-lah-h h h h h h h h h h hh h h h h h h h h!
May you be inscribed for life in the New Year!

THE REDEEMER

Disguised as a humble, unknown Jew,
a learned rabbi, a beloved teacher,
a doctor who performs medical miracles,
he heals the sick.
He travels through the valley of the shadow
of death.
He wanders over the earth
bound by neither time nor space.
No one knows who he really is.
He appears in many disguises--
Elijah, the messenger,
warning, advising in times of distress
bringing consolation to the afflicted,
Elijah, enduring hopeful.

On Passover, we open the door
for Elijah to enter.
The fifth cup of wine is poured for him
near a bowl of the bitter tears
our ancestors shed on their flight
from Egypt.
Year after year we open the door
for the spirit of Elijah to enter
to celebrate the Passover Seder with
families all over the world--

Elijah, worker of miracles
Elijah, performer of wonders,
Elijah, the healer
Elijah, the prophet
Elijah, the peacemaker
Elijah, the arbitrator
Elijah, the provider
Elijah, protector of children
Elijah, the magician
Elijah, the Tishbite
Elijah, the Gileadite

Eliahu, ha-navi
Eliahu, ha-Tishbi,
Eliahu, Eliahu, Eliahu
ha-Giladi.

Elijah, transcribed to heaven
in a chariot of fire!

UNGRASPABLE REALITY

My dialogue with God became a monologue dragging
a burning bush and a pillar of fire across
mountains and seas.
I waited for Him on clouds in all conditions for so long
the many dimensions of space became
hopelessly scrambled.
Left and right, up and down, before and after
lost their meaning.
In the vast universe of vibrating strings the equations
blew up in my face.
In the grand swirl of galaxies populated by strange
and abstract ideas
chance replaced logic and the universe chose its own
boundaries never finished or fixed.
I grappled with the cataclysms of time and space
and what it is to live on a knife edge
where matter is ruled by probability on the verge
of eternal expansion or virtual collapse.
I saw into a realm of experience that defies the idea
of location.
I saw the interconnectedness of all things and that
hope and renewal in word and deed
may involve an entire people down through the ages
and that there was a desert made Eden
and that the Kabbalists and mystics of the world
knew something we do not.

THE LEGACY

I awake and everything happens all over again.
Grandma hobbles out with bones and skin
to stretch and yawn.
The darkness is reborn, but it has never been
so dark.
Grandma recites the *Hashkivenu*:
"Help us, O God, to lie down in peace."
The dead rise to their feet and begin praying.
It is evening and it is morning.
Someone is arguing in a strange language.
Grandma is plucking feathers.
Mother is silent. She shrinks into herself
like *dagesh*, a little dot,
while I, *yud*, the smallest letter, hang
suspended from the body of the *aleph*.
Mother is yoked to the pull of the generations.
I am held fast by *yad chazaka*, a strong hand.
Vav is the sound of our being joined
to the generations of women who belong to
past and future.
Dalet is the door through which we must go.
Great-grandma guards *beyt*, the house of
beginning.

CAN A FIG GROW?

I stare into a dull, tarnished mirror.
I trace the afflictions of old age
on my face.
Can a fig grow from a thorn?
Can a rose blossom from a thistle?

The landscape is frosted over.
My goal is unclear, to be reached by
paths undefined.
Inside the letters of the alphabet
I am a silent letter, a wounded vowel
echoing.

Like a candle that stretches with its
flame
I let myself go.
I hear Sarah's laughter in my heart.
The sun climbs and warms
to this vision.

I put earth in my shoes, some crystal
in my mouth
to make my speech true.
I toast tomorrow with white wine from
Germany
tasting of resurrection.

THE STRENGTH TO ENDURE

Against an exuberant excess of colors
and forms
we assess the weight and shape of
our words from science, scripture
and speculation.
Survivors of an ancient culture
still worshipping the God
of the ten commandments
we remove from the Ark the Torah scrolls
dressed in colorful velvet
with their sterling silver breastplates
and silver pointers.
Silence is filled with metaphysical
speculation.
We keep our amazement
our eagerness alive.
The choir sings choral music
with a cantus firmus,
a ground bass--
the basso obligato,
an incessant repetition of our will
to survive

CLIMBING

Let us look for roads and crossroads
where extremes not only meet,
they follow each other in the fiery
glow of daylight breaking.
Let us speak of roads and highways
and how the road climbs the hill
shaking with exhaustion
but climb the hill it must.
The air is full of promise.
The sky is a porcelain cup filled
with butterflies.
Against the blue of the cloudless sky
I, too, climb and climb
blinded by a brilliant shaft
of sunlight
as the sun climbs and warms
the land
in the presence of the sea
with all my life spread out before me
for which no words can be found.

DIVINE THREADS

I write this book with the abiding faith
of a visionary
I weave several threads of hope
in humankind--
divine threads radiating anticipations
throwing sparks of fire flying out
from the last chapters of my life
like this book not yet signed,
sealed and delivered to the Publisher.
I open the Book of Divine Letters
representing numbers and sounds--
the whole heaven a musical scale
of harmony and melody
while the shocking and horrific
chords of dissonance
expressed in the sacrifice of millions
of lives lost in the evil and depraved
years of the Holocaust, turn
my days and nights
into a blazing Havdalah candle
made up of enduring strands of
love.
I merge with the Source
holding in my hands the fire that
does not forget the ash.

QUESTIONING GOD

WHAT GOD IS THIS WHO ELUDES REVELATION AND COMMUNICATION?

What God is this who eludes revelation
and communication?
What God is this whose mountain of holiness
is surrounded by a harsh and terrible
cloud of silence?
Whose God is this who requires no partner
from whom to receive a reply, even
in the shadow of Auschwitz?
What God is this who comes from too far away
to keep watch?
Whose God is this whose most challenging form
of silence is flight?
Who is this God whose silence is a place
of extreme aggression,
whose silence at critical moments is
worse than contempt?
Who is this God whose reality can never be
verified or challenged
even when, from the *tephillin* box
strapped to the forehead of religious men
praying,
the letters forming the *Shema* ascend to Him?
Whose God is this in revolt,
strong willed to the point of petulance?
Who is this God who runs aground on the shoals
of His own need to topple things and create
chaos
while every blade of grass has its angel
that bends over it and whispers, "Grow, grow"?[1]
What God is this who accepts burnt offerings
of human flesh with analytical detachment?
Who is this God who saw a black star painted
over the left breast of the sky
and said nothing?
Whose God disappears while holy men pray
with a concentration that absorbs all

contradiction
while chunks of landscape turn red
with the blood of the innocent?

WHAT IF GOD'S FINGERS ARE LIMP AND UNWILLING?

What if God's fingers are limp and unwilling
to grasp my thoughts
that have no equivalent in words?
What if God holds all the big cosmic riddles
in His hands without letting go?
What if He were endowed with my breath
and my being?
What if He were my Muse with a divine life
of her own?
What if He were the Child-Maiden,
the All-giving Mother, the angry Crone
in any order or simultaneously?

WHY DOES GOD REFUSE TO REVEAL HER BEING ?

Why does God refuse to reveal Her Being
and I, I have constantly to gamble
on her Seeming, asking myself,
have I taken as real
that which is perhaps only appearance?
One can never tell when the word
is pretending
or when it is serious.
The word betrays the Ineffable
embracing the Infinite.
But when the chords of two instruments
are in harmony
then it is enough if one vibrates
for the other to sing.

REFLECTIONS ON THE NINTH DAY OF AV

The ninth day of Av--the day of mourning
for the destruction of the Temple in Jerusalem
and the exile of the Jewish people--
a symbol of all persecutions of Jews.
The sanctuary is draped in black.
The ark is draped in black.
Recalling this calamitous day the rabbi reads
from the Book of Lamentations.
How can he explain the many persecutions
that have befallen the Jews?
Some say God is a God of wrath and retribution
a God of conflict between opposites.
Some say God hides and reveals Himself.
In truth, that is His terrible dilemma.
His divided nature is the tragedy of God.
Shma Yisrael Adonai Elohaynu, Adonai echad.
Father of Mercies, where were You when my people
set out in families on the road to extermination?

The moon hangs low like a mutilated scroll lowered
for burial in the cemetery.
Again I hear Your voice ringing through the graves:
"And I will give you new heart and spirit,
seasons of happiness, holidays of joy!"
I turn to the unrest in the Jewish soul,
to the recurrent cry of the persecuted and the oppressed.
I hear my people in me struggling for a voice.
Oh, compassionate God, our Fortress, our Deliverer,
why didn't the "Thirty-Six Righteous Men"
save the Jews from annihilation in the Holocaust?
Did You grieve, *Hashem*, for each life that was lost?
Stained with the blood and tears of our martyrs
we petition You again for protection and peace.
We beseech You, *Hashem*. We are sorely afflicted.
Will You save us now? If not now, when?

THE FINGERPRINTS OF DARK ENERGY

Before God created the world
time did not exist.
There was no time before that.
There was no "then" then.
What was God doing in the primordial
Nothingness
and for how long?
We embrace yet constantly quarrel
with the Divine.
In the gap between faith and reason
we yearn for a glimpse of
a higher moral order
but we stumble like fools
mired in excrement.
God's apocalyptic decrees collide
with our scientific inquiries.
While we gather together
black holes and string theories
we fall deeper into sinkholes
of biological and chemical waste.
We span vast cosmological distances
but we never stop wondering
if creation took place
in a stupendously tiny length
of eternity
like a billionth of a trillionth
of a centimeter of time.

WHO WILL SAVE THE BRANCHES OF THE TREE OF LIFE FROM DESTRUCTION?

I wander through legends of the Hasidic masters
as I listen to a Jewish song of lament on an old,
discarded, long-playing record.
"*Eli, Eli*... my God, my God, why hast Thou
forsaken me?"
There was no answer then or now.
Waves of fire surge through explosions
on a cosmic scale in the Book of Formation.
Branches of the Tree of Life sway
and fall.
Who will pluck them out of the fire?
Whose kingdom come
Whose will be done on earth
as it is in heaven?

THE QUANTUM PHYSICIST AND GOD

He studied the physics of the very small.
He opened a notebook and began his feverish
calculations.
In the process of numbers adding up
he found logic replaced by chance
and matter ruled by probability
but he could find no language adequate
to describe parameters of the infinitely
small
connecting everything to everything else
in the universe--
peculiarly, singularly, astonishingly
radical
turning the infinitude of the small
into an entity of vastness and immensity.

What set this conception in motion?
The Unexplainableness?
The Inconceivability?
The Indescribability?
Is ambiguity one of the attributes of God?
God, the Equivocal?
God, the Incomprehensible?
The Unfathomable?
The Impenetrable?
The Inscrutable?
Are these the names of God?
Are names a way to lay fingers on God
in metaphor, in apologue?

Did a gargantuan blast create the universe?
Did it start out the size of a marble
or a grapefruit?
Confronted by question after question
obscured by multiplicity,
is there an underlying simplicity,
a single force that is fundamental to
the universe?

What if the solid geometry of space is
held in place by the shifting identities of
God's names cemented together
with a quark-gluon plasma?
Where are His remaining names?
God of Compassion!
God of Love!
Can God overcome his dissociative
amnesia?
When we ask the most daunting of
questions
why does God turn into a veil?

SPIRITUAL CANTICLE

In the vaulted immensity of the sky
the old stars go out one by one.
The galaxies move apart from
each other.
Space grows emptier.
Was there a beginning?
Will there be an end?
Did the universe begin suddenly?
If there was a beginning
what came before?
When all the stars go out
what will come after
the holy seas
the sacred earth
the green journeys of our growth?
What will be when God enters
into Himself again
and refuses to come out
and *Binah*,[1] our mother, is nowhere
to be found
and the light contracts into a
hand's breadth
and time is reduced to the pinhead
of a moment
and what should be weighty in the
mouth is light?
Is there a weep-hole for the rumblings
and tumblings of war in our
plundered world?
Will a torn-off shred of Eden
melt bullets
and the ice on tears
of lead?

BINAH
(Understanding)

The trees stand in leaf and the hills rise up green
to meet them.
We lift up our eyes to the distant hills.
From whence cometh our help?
Where is wisdom glowing with light radiating
from the last hours of daylight?
Morning rises from the mists of night.
A staff brings forth blossoms and produces
almonds.
Under a tree I read from the book of *Yashar*.
In its pages the whole Torah is one line.
I dream of *Adahm* and *Chava*,
the first man and woman
and the *Yetser Harah*,
the Evil Inclination in the form of *Nachash*,
the crafty serpent who maimed them into truth.
So also are we maimed in our fall from darkness
to light.
We, too, have missed the mark.
Our perception remains flawed and inadequate
before the hidden Intelligence from beyond
this world.
What does it mean, the cry of a rain of leaves?
The laugh of split boulders?
The trees clad only in their bare branches?
We knock on the seven gates of wisdom.
Satan, the tester, blocks our way.
What does it mean, the willingness of Abraham,
the readiness of Isaac?
We stand in a field of holy apple trees eating
apples.
We stand face to face under showers of leaves.
A little wind springs up overwhelming in its
understatement.
Something is growing and deepening and
overflowing.

THROUGH THE HALF-OPENED WINDOWS
OF LIFE IN JEOPARDY

Through the half-opened windows of life in jeopardy
I look out on a garden of decapitated trees.
The mourning of a ram's horn breaks the silence.
Heavenly Father, why have evil men manufactured
a rope with which they want to hang us
and this message like a letter of last reprieve,
will be picked up, pocketed and lost.
Why is dark green spring steeped in silence?
Why are innocent people punished like sinners
in Gehenna, half in fire, half in snow?

Is evil something we must learn to live with?
Did the seeds of the apple from the Garden of Eden
grow the tree that was used for the cross?
The road to war is covered with blood.
The world has shrunk until it is nothing more than
a line around my feet.
Under a stretch of overcast sky I stumble
on an old charred, burnt-out pit.
I think of shoes that were once piled high
and faces pressed to rain-drenched windows.

I fling open the windows looking out on life.
The Bible affirms, "The blood is the life."[1]
It states: "In your blood, live!"[2]
Tchernikovsky said, "Each man with his pain
and each with his deformity."
Let the homeless, the poor, the orphaned
children of the world find love and acceptance
as they re-establish their lives
empowered and confident of survival
and growth.
Not for nothing are these words spoken.

WHO MAPPED THE STARS?

Who mapped the stars in monuments of stone?
Was it the lunar Librarian who invented
hieroglyphics
and threw them at me in a game of catch?
Did the lunar Librarian invent
the dialectic of the sea that pulls itself
toward me and away from me
like a swing flying through the air?

Who invented the first letter *aleph*
and the final letter *tav*?
But of all the letters of the alphabet
I run toward *het*.
It resembles a gate.
I dance through it from one life to another.
Like an underground detector,
my mind keeps searching for the elusive
neutrino of creative thought
that changes form as it flies through
matter.

Like an editor molecule it causes
the DNA of a poem and its coding to change
its written message
even as it is being written,
determining even, how the message of
the coding is to be read,
whether in the original or the edited
version.
It happens suddenly when the Muse turns
absurdity into reality
and offers shape and beauty to new
ways of seeing.

THE ILLUMINATED JOURNEY

TEARING YOURSELF LOOSE

If you are an edge-dweller in a world
where ruptures and discontinuities
run deep,
the edge will crumble under your feet
like a trail of light burning out
from friction
unless you ride the River of No Return,
I mean ride it, while it rages
like a seething maelstrom
as you squeeze through the strait
called Impassable Canyon
dropping down between boulders
where there is little breathing room,
holding fast to your raft called
Last Chance
and with your talent for direction-
finding
and landmark-spotting
thrust yourself through swirling
floodwaters
as the river shudders through its entire
length.
The voyage itself is liberating
and empowering
but the River of No Return will not
trace its old course.
It zigs and zags,
loops and dips.
Thrown off the raft by lashing waves
you wait at the river's edge for your raft
to float by
so you can swim out to it and continue
your journey to a chancy destination
where you, a drenched woman, were
shaken free
to commune with the river, the wind
and the sea.

BREAKTHROUGH

The phosphorescent river was bathed in a wash
of gold, silver and coppery light.
Its surface was encrusted with diamonds
and pearls.
We followed its moody, mystical turns.
The river spoke loudly and softly,
quickly and slowly.
At times it sang mysterious litanies.
Out of a steep canyon it ran
fast toward the rapids.
Plunging into the waters we took a wrong turn
as the river divided.
Our raft caught a ledge that tumbled us
into churning water.
We were swept down to the next rapid and into
a whirlpool that held us under water
and tumbled us so violently
it tore the clothes right off our backs.
We fought the waves downstream.
The river was on a rampage.
It expanded in convulsive fury.
It headed for the rocks.
Then the water embraced us like a purifying
baptism.
We swam toward shore.
The wind wound and unwound the clouds
as if they were threads on the loom
of the sky.
It was night. It was day.
The moon's melon-belly hung like fruit
above our heads.
In the presence of an Intelligence
and a mystery
we climbed out of the river
at World's End
holding fast to the winding-rope
of prayer
aflame with sunlight.

RAFTING UP PASSION RIVER

El Penitente rafts up Passion River
singing deep laments so compelling
they transcend time and place.
He sets out on foot up a steep,
narrow path to a clearing of
forest.
He traces a lost world of stelae,
altars, glyphs and stone carvings.
Its dangers, its beauty, its indwelling,
its allure, lead to a violent,
calamitous sight--
a sea with no horizon and a sky
fractured with angled masts.
Indifferent to the site of fears
and fantasies, the angled masts
set sail for the Port of Last Resort.
Angels walk there with hems
lightly lifted.
As morning rips the purple off
the sky
El Penitente glows with joy
and beatitude.

WORLD'S END

You are getting ready to take a trip
to Always.
You don't expect to spend
the rest of your life there.
You are at a bend of the river
known as World's End.
You row through fog to catch the
first light.
Is Always a magical place
or a never-ending journey to the
Everlasting?

Why does the present act out the myth
of the past
as though all your odysseys were
Homer's Odyssey?
And is the legacy of the Odyssey
a belief in the reality of
an imperishable love
far beyond the full measure of
your days?

CHANGE

I remember things before they happen
the way a blind woman feels things

all the hidden edges and ends of things
tearing loose from their moorings

carrying me along like a haunting raga
that will never leave you.

This is the point of no return
the place we have come to.

We enter it the way a river enters the sea
with the voice of a great rushing.

I look at you receding and receding
like lost music.

You wave goodbye to me
until I am a speck on the horizon.

Tomorrow another sun will come up
out of a river of song with no banks.

THE SEA IS THUNDERING IN A WHITE MAELSTROM

The sea is thundering in a white maelstrom
of foam.
I am far from any ocean,
yet I feel the salt of fresh sea air
on my face
and the hot, baked sand under my feet.
I hear the slap of waves,
the surging music of the swell
like a sibylline whisper,
the running tide boiling and hissing
and the sea forever thundering.
Listen.

THE ILLUMINATED JOURNEY

We sailed past the Islands of Doubt.
The compass needle we were told to
follow to guide our boat kept slipping
away.
We applied more and more rudder
as we came up into the wind.
The sails backed off as the wind
struck from the wrong side
of the boat.
The rigging slapped about.
The prayerful part of our lives moved
farther away.
As we lost headway, the Captain,
thoroughly alarmed, came out on deck
to guide the wheel.
He moved the craft into a bay of
smooth water.
Gulls poured out their gullish songs
as they wandered the skies.
Bestowing on ourselves a priestly
blessing
beginning with the word
Yevarechecha,
we set sail toward unlimited
possibilities
like a spark in search of its flame
charting our journey of
the spirit
in the presence of a single gleam
of light.

YOU CANNOT TURN BACK

Once you have left an old way of life
and crossed a sea of commitment
and contemplation
you cannot turn back, for in life
every stage is part of a sacred journey.
So when you are called
to an intimate connectedness
with the Other
doors will open for you unexpectedly
from one life into another
some real, some imaginary.

Another time that has broken through
will send you reeling
but you will come to terms
with your past
and the old will be made new
and the new made unforgettable
through this indissoluble bond
this complex dialogue
that defies analysis
and that leaves the mystery
intact.

AN ANCIENT CITY IS THERE IN MY DREAMS

An ancient city is there in my dreams,
where I don't know
but I can go, I will find it--
my legendary city of dreams.

I follow signs and portents through
medieval gates, ruined arches,
broken fountains, fragments
of walls.

I follow old routes toward Carthage
and Xanadu,
Safed, Petra, Lhaza, Ectabana,
Athens, Jaffa,
Jerusalem and Jericho

to Doric columns that were once
a great temple,
to time and space interrelated
for everything is in everything else.

My city is there in the holy places,
where, I don't know
but I can go, I *will* find it
in the begettings and births
that call me forth.

IT IS DIFFICULT TO TAKE THE JOURNEY ALONE

It is difficult to take the journey
alone.
The highway is full of detours.
There are sharp curves in the road,
endless construction causing
traffic slow-downs and tie-ups,
cars funneling into one lane
and fender-benders.

The journey takes me through
the rowdy reds and yellows
of summer's decline,
the wine colors of autumn,
the soft tints and half-tints of Titian
and winter's vistas of unearthly
grandeur
where all songs are absorbed
in silence
and the stars glitter.

In the autumn of my years
I am learning how the maple leaves
are harvesting sunlight
and how a different destiny
is working itself out,
different and yet the same
and I am learning to read messages
written in vanishing ink
and that your door is open
and you are waiting for me.

MEDITATIONS

I THINK OF YOU

In my thoughts and feelings, I pray
at the grave of Rachel, our mother
and at the graves of the righteous
on the Mount of Olives.
I pray in a quorum of ten, wrapped
in prayer shawl and *kittel.*
I climb up to the roof of an Israeli
house where I can see
Lake Kinneret in the distance.
I recite the prayer of the Casting
and I think of you, my dearest
ones.
During the closing of the gates
at the time the sun is sinking over
the treetops
during the hour when the judgment
is sealed,
I think of all mankind.
When the *Tekiah, Shevarim, Teruah*
ring out loud and clear
and the closing prayer is still being
prayed on Yom Kippur
and it is finished
with the coming out of the stars,
I think of you, dearest ones.

THE SABBATH BRIDE IS A LAUGHING GIRL

The Sabbath Bride is a laughing girl
dressed in white garments.
She stands in the reddish light of
the sunset.
Peace flows from her parted lips.
The Garden enters with her.
Mother lights the candles, covers her eyes
with the palms of her hands and recites
the benediction.
Father chants the blessing over wine
and says *ha-motzi*
placing ten fingers on the bread.
Rebecca, Rachel and Leah gather around.
They have come from afar, Sarah, also,
from the cave of Machpelah.
They savor the sweet odors of mother's
cooking.
They pray in a *minyan* with other women
from sundown to sundown.
When the rejoicing Bride tears herself away
with all the Sabbath souls trailing after her,
the ancestral Matriarchs vanish like breath
from the face of a mirror.

NOTES TRICKLE FROM MY FINGERS

Notes trickle from my fingers.
There is the palpable sense of the sea
all around me,
yet I remember the music as if it were
yesterday--
a fugue of breathtaking, virtuosic
proportions,
such is the rhythm of the color
and massing.
Such are the themes.
Such is the dialogue between two voices.
Such is the sequential unfolding
in real time.
The voices continue to interweave
in search of one another.
Whichever melody is dominant
whichever one holds sway
the other continues softly
never entirely fading away.

THE DAY OF JUDGMENT LAYS BARE

The day of judgment lays bare
the structure of the soul.
The Shofar begins with short,
plaintive sounds.
Who shall come to a timely end
and who shall come to an
untimely end?
Who shall be lowered and who
shall be raised?
How many shall pass away
and how many shall be born?
Who, blotted out of the Book
of Life?
Who, written in, in a firm hand?
Hear the plain *tekiah* that ends
abruptly.
Hear the broken *shevarim*.
the three short sounds.
Hear the *teruah*, the succession
of tremulous notes equal to
three *shevarim*.
Hear the *tekiah gedolah-h-h-h-h-h-h-h*
the greatly prolonged *tekiah*.
With these sounds I am purified
and awakened, filled with awe
before the wonder of faith
holding steady in the face of
human finitude,
filled with hope as huge as a
galaxy of blazing spheres
shedding light,
filled with love, large, great
and inconceivable,
beyond all thought and imaging.

THE LIGHT STREAMS OUT

And there we are, holding a burning
and shining lamp
to lives we don't know in far-away places
where the rain is beating down
on graves with no markers.

And there we are, speaking a language
we did not know we knew
while the word "holy" is repeated
three times
and old prayer-books
with their inscrutable mysteries
are hidden from view.

And there we are, with fresh challenges
to meet
as we sit in our aloneness and speak
to our ancestors
who can only be imagined
and relatives we remember for
life.

The mystery of unknowing bites
its mark in us
as we carry our dead relatives
in our thoughts.
No matter how different their lives
from ours
there is an indestructible bond of
comedic awareness, tolerance
and admiration
big enough to stretch beyond biology
and across time.

TRUTH IN THE EXILIC MODE

Exiled from the spiritual life
of my innermost being
why do I wait for a special time
that never arrives
to turn the everydayness
of every day
into a conflagration?
My thoughts and feelings
ignite like timber
from combustible materials
that rage and explode.
I know the way out of
years of drought
is through a firestorm of
biblical proportions
and what trickles down as ash
or rain
will find its way up.

TRUTH IN THE RHAPSODIC MODE

O, Abulafia,[1] the Hebrew letters
cast an endless spell.
I follow the twists and turns
of the letters.
In each square letter is a tiny seed.
In each seed is a *yod*
through which creation enters.
A fiery wind shakes up the letters embracing
God's radiance in exile.
Ahava raba. Chemla gedola.
With abiding love, with boundless love--
I stop to catch my breath.
The alphabet letters are flying to new heights.
Mood is frail, transient, open to
change and transmutation
but above the full moon high
and white in the sky
truth in the rhapsodic mode
prevails in quiet joy
with a raised hand pointing to God.

TRUTH IN THE MIDRASHIC MODE

I dreamed my bookcases were thrown out of a window
and all my books fell to the ground.
The wind scattered the loose pages.
They circled my head like a bride circling her groom
seven times.

I scooped up a fiercely visionary work
scanning the lines with their torn letters,
their missing phrases, their truths, perplexities
and contradictions.

I held in my hands the broken shapes, lines,
forms, textures and perspectives--
the hardness, softness, roundness, straightness,
the sharpness, lightness, opacity--
all that wanted to be said.

I had trouble recognizing half-obliterated words,
blurred letters and broken connections.
The text itself kept disappearing
like drowned spires in a watery landscape.

Then the text emerged, Beethovenian
in outpouring,
Brahmsian in grandeur,
Chopinesque in beauty.
I woke with my rescued books before me.

I woke blessed to absorb many teachings.
I woke like an undreamed-of consonant
in an undreamed-of world.
I woke in the garden that entered with me.

I woke with bells ringing
wildly swinging
crashing into each other
in a mass of chords
in clashing melodies

ringing out in dissonant harmony
rebounding and echoing

and the voice of a lamp
and the air damp
with the smell of salt
in the sea air
as a great peace flowed
into me.

TRUTH IN THE MODE OF PSYCHOLOGY AND INTUITION

*"What a blessing it is to love books as I love
them-- and to live amidst the unreal!"*
                            -- Macaulay

We live in a world where lives are books
and books are lives
transforming love and sexuality
into a search for knowledge.
We touch the skin of the erotic
and magical, a teasing foreplay--
a seduction, a summoning.
Love arranged the words from
a dictionary of sounds
and opened new channels of
communication.

There were images woven on the dream-loom.
There was decentering and displacement,
the search for the unknowable and
the out of reach,
a shifting of moods of alarm, surprise,
bewilderment and joy,
extravagant gestures and contemplation.
Zen teaches that when we are most aware
there is no feeling of separation
between subject and object.

Still, questions occurred as we acknowledged
the pile-up of associations
activating our metaphors.
Blocked by self-doubt we can no longer invite
ourselves
to enter the space of an invented persona
or to find a pen that writes truthfully,
yet, in the language of gestures,
we continue to write.

Every word launched is a leap of faith,
every safe landing a victory.
We are astonished to discover that
we have the courage to take risks
for our work
and to keep our footing on a glass mountain
for we are part of something
larger than ourselves--
the poem's transformative power,
its ability to create new ways of being
for at any given moment several realities
are going on at once all tangled up together
often glaringly contradictory
or even more confusing, juxtaposed
side by side, or in alternation,
or so tightly interwoven as to be
indistinguishable.

Like music shimmering with liquid warmth
and as personal as vibrato
on a violin
we embrace our opposing selves and recreate
our solo parts
for our hearts are stretched just wide enough
to accept ambivalence as a creative force
and to embrace contradiction
so we won't have to weave the tapestry
of our words
day after day after day after day
and unravel it at night.

A BLUE SCROLL UNWINDING

The past reached out like an unseen hand
and grasped me by the hair of my head.
It carried me as God once clasped
and carried Ezekiel in the land of the
Chaldeans.
As it lifted sinew, bone and prayer
my words fell away.
The horizon offered itself
on all sides,
a blue scroll unwinding its galaxy
of prophets.
One of the prophets reached out to me
and said:
Do not mourn words.
Like the poor who are given the gleanings
of the field,
the forgotten sheaves of grain--
you shall be given the leftover corners
of the field of remembrance.
Say the blessings over wine and spices
for a fragrant week,
then light at sundown, a long white candle
in memory of Adam.

LIFE OF THE LETTERS

Can you hear the music of the letters of the alphabet?
Listen to it
and follow it into the darkness that precedes creation.
Like scrolls of the Torah the letters assemble into waves
rolling out into the world through the generations.
They rise into a great yearning wave covering the centuries.
As the waters recede each letter becomes a tree of knowledge
that bears fruit.
The letters dwell in their names like the heads of giraffes
nuzzling among leaves.
Each is peculiarly haunting and has about it a magic spell.
The letters capture the susurrus of waves yet they thunder
with the voice of the lion of Judah.
Each is a seraph with his fiery coal cleansing the heart.
Each letter is the horn of a Jewish unicorn[1] purifying
thought
Each has a *neshamah* reaching up to its proper place,
the great Sinai of faith, even the little letter *aleph*.
Each follows the cycle of Torah readings that ends and begins,
ends and begins.
The letters pour down in torrents. All begins over again.
And God said *Devarim*. These are the words that have
neither
beginning nor end.
Holy holy holy are the sparks of the alphabet's letters.

PSALM OF THANKSGIVING

How like nothing on earth you are, God,
and yet your presence is everywhere
for you are the Origin
the Source of all.
All that dies above or below
renews itself,
each stone, each river, each flower,
each tree
remembers the blueprint.
Stars, planets, die and are reborn.
Your formlessness gives birth to form.
Had I eyes to see far off
Had I eyes to see near
Had I eyes to see the shapes and colors
of your design
had I ears to hear melodies intertwined
the rhythms, the harmonies in every song
sung
could I but comprehend everything
unfolding
my heart would fly like a tornado
on the loose
my mind would arch forward in a
gesture of offering
and my soul, in joy, would lie back
across the body of the universe
before the wonder of it all.

GOD OF PERPETUITY,
IF YOU SHOULD CALL ME

God of Perpetuity, if you should call me,
I will transform myself into a receptive
vessel.
Prove me, God, and you will know
my heart.
From the thunder of your Voice that sent
landslides of fear down the slopes
of Mount Sinai,
I stand before You in my world of missed
opportunities and fading hopes.
I remember when I was like Moses leading
the ragged people of my thoughts
and feelings
through the wilderness of sinful
transgressions.
I was reluctant to show them the Tablets
of your Law
for they danced around the Golden Calf
but like you, God,
I forgive them for their faithlessness.
I forgive myself
for my transgressions.

IN THE GRANDEUR OF EVOLUTION

I, a voluptuary of words, open the
Book Of Letters
representing numbers and sounds.
The night sky glows like a magic
onyx.
In its black depths are points of
light.
I am pregnant with language, ready
to deliver.
Fragments of a rainbow join together.
Shoals of clouds shift among reefs.
Moons, stars and suns are born
in the galaxies.
They die when their time is up.
For now, here on earth, the shadowy
mysticism and incantatory power
of my massive oak tree with its wide
arms reach out and embrace me.
Its leafy branches touch
the other side of Highland Avenue.
On summer nights, fireflies flash
codes of light to other fireflies.
In the neon-orange light of a new dawn
the green lion of summer swallows
the flaming sun.

REMEMBER THE LIGHT

Before the sun sets and the valley is filled
with the shadow of death,
before night descends, remember the light
which wanders from one end of the world
to the other.
Remember the *Ner Tamid*,
the eternal light burning before the ark
in the temple.
Remember the Sabbath candles glowing
on Friday night.
Remember the lighted menorah
on the joyful nights of Chanukah.
Bread and wine, joy and learning intertwine
struggling with darkness like Jacob who
wrestled with an angel
through the shadowy night.
Light pours in through the windows
of the sanctuary transforming
the ordinary into a soulbird descending
from a great height.

COME, MY BELOVED

The sun is going down in the redness cast
by mountains of fire and hills of flame.
Dusk lifts its pointer of light.
Mother chants the blessing as she lights
the candles after sunset.
The twisted loaves are on the table,
the stuffed fish bound up with God.
The red wine is ready to be poured
to celebrate the day which is more than
a day.
This is the love for that which is yet
unborn.
Quiet joy. Candles flickering. A star lit
against the soft twilight.
A great quietness.
Night falls like the wing of a nesting
bird.
Come, my Beloved, come, Bride of God,
shy Bride of a day
on this quiet evening of Sabbath joy
and sanctified rest.

BEYOND FLESH TO FLESH COUPLING

I taught you that the eternal Thou
is the supreme partner in our dialogue
making a marriage between spirit
and flesh.
I taught you to understand the gifts
I shared with you
and my need now to say what I left
unspoken.
I taught you that love finds in the
intrinsic beauty of an intimate
relationship nurtured with kindness
and compassion
love without any conditions at all.

I showed you that life begins to decay
when we fail to sense
the grandeur of what is eternal
in time
and that the divine Spirit gives many
blessings
but that salvation is a work-in-progress.
I helped you to see that infinite love
is firmly earthbound
in deeds of kindness and generosity.
I taught you there is surprise and terror
in sadness and loss.
I helped you to understand the difference
between a love song and a swan song.

OPENING A LINE OF COMMUNICATION

The veils and rings are gone.
The *chuppah* poles are gone.
Phylacteries wound around the head
are gone.
The garden walls are shrouded.
The floriferous fairy roses are dead.
Bellini and Puccini are dead.
Mounds of books, unread, sink
into remainders
while boundless, formless, infinite,
eternal undivided Reality
above, below and on every side opens
a line of communication with
the Archangel, Chamuel, Seer of God,
Jophiel, the Beauty of God
and Zadkiel the justice of God.

FORGIVENESS AND UNDERSTANDING

On Rosh Hashanah and Yom Kippur
memory is the key to salvation.
Let us use it to get at the heart
of things,
to unlock the past that goes back
to the beginning.
Let us sweep up all the dust from
the mind's corners.
Let our hearts be filled to overflowing
by the spirit of the prophets.
Let faith lead us into the Holy of
Holies.
A white curtain is spread over the
Ark of the Covenant.
White covers cover the Torah Scrolls.
Let the whiteness of forgiveness
fill our souls
as full of understanding as the ocean
is filled with water.

I GIVE THANKS

I feel the moist warm breath of July
in the air.
The long shadow of a great oak tree
rolls across my front lawn.
As the wind rises the tree shakes
its limbs back and forth
swaying and dancing.
The sun shines like the perpetual lamp
that burns before the Ark.
I give thanks for this day, quiet
in my gratitude.
I give thanks for the moon
rising after sundown
resplendent in its gold and crimson
velvet.
Night enters through the gates
of my back lawn
as it does through the gates of
Jerusalem
and over the ruins of Ephesus
in Turkey
and over the threads and tatters,
the fables of my life
moving beyond boundaries
and definitions
to the path of no return,
death.
I give thanks for all I have been
blessed to receive
and for my mind still active
in the life of the spirit.

BEARING FRUIT

I observe how space flows with time
as I walk a tricky line between
doubt and certainty.
A century old pear tree is bearing
fruit
but Venus, above me, to the left,
is setting too quickly
even as the roses in my garden bloom
incandescently red.
At my most inwardly passionate
I live my final days in total combustion
while the *Finale* of my life
writes itself out
with a moral imperative
like a *Grosse Fugue*.

TRANSFORMED INTO A BOOK OF LOVE

Where do space and time begin?
They work their design
into everything, holding locked
secrets and paradoxes
and the clue to the mystery of
God--the identity of the
Nothingness that was, that is
and always will be, that Einstein
called Force, that keeps
the universes and galaxies on
course
and Earth from spinning out of
orbit.

And what of the gravitational pull
of an old soul
to a psychological penetration
that seems preternatural
in which all times are the same time
and all places the same place
everywhere--and here, right now
like an eternal Presence?

ROOT OF ALL ROOTS

O, Abulafia,[1] where are the circles within circles in the hidden circles in the life of this world? How shall I find even one little circle, that my hand might reach out to the circumference of my days and joyfully turn the letters of the alphabet and combine them in the ways of wisdom?

What of the rims and spokes leading to the center of *ayin*? How shall I hold fast to them and find buried seeds of light as I journey from circle into circle of the world I live in following the many paths of the letters?

O, the clear strokes and slashes of the Hebrew letters. O, heavenly angel, Metatron, your letters hang from the branches of the ancient tree of life! In each of your letters is a tiny seed. in each seed a *yod* through which creation enters. The light streams out. In the mouth of night a mighty wind shakes the letters. They whirl away.

The letters hover above a wilderness of parchment in a blizzard of black letters spreading in circles. They embrace God's radiance in exile. Will the search for a new beginning be prolonged forever? The letters roll and lift themselves above silver pointers. Will the Tree of Knowledge of Good and Evil regain its lost lights?

O, Abulafia, in the light's dazzling climb to the uppermost heaven, the letters form a ladder out of roots and tongues. They stand, head close to head, peering with dark eyes. They reach up higher and higher to the crown of the sky, each letter a gleaming light that will not die.

They create their own Paradise in prayer from Sabbath to Sabbath, released from the world of toil. They are a Garden of Eden, a song lifted up, full of the Indwelling Presence, full of *aleph*, the Source.

The letters form unshakable pillars of faith. *Ahava raba, chemla gedola* with abounding love, with great compassion, they sustain the whole world from the middle pillar of the *Shema* outward.

THE CLOUDS ARE WALKING

The clouds are walking the sky
in billowy clothes.
They are dressed in festive white
garments like the vestments
worn on Yom Kippur.
Here on the ground I hear
the rustle of things growing.
The day is huge.
Shadows crouch under the trees
with their quiet birds.
I look with the enlarging gaze
of a small girl.
With the heart of a little child
I look at humankind
still trying to put together
the letters on the shattered
tables of the covenant.
When will all people be helped?
All illnesses wiped out?
The clouds are walking the sky
all over the world.
On the ground I hear the rustle
of things growing.

FULL OF THE FLIGHT OF BIRDS

We stand motionless feeling the
warmth of the sun
against the blue of the sky.
The grass waves in the wind.
We are out in the open
in blinding sunlight
on the edge of an immense clearing.
A whole multitude of birds
envelops us.
We tumble like chips in a rolling
barrel.
The wind is in our pocket.
We are full of the flight of birds
freed, liberated.

THE SPIRIT OF LOVE FLOWS EVERYWHERE

The spirit of love flows everywhere
flows in a vast and limitless expanse
flows beyond all boundaries
flows into the silence and quietude
of night
flows in sparks of sunlight
flows into jars and bricks
flows into the root of the light
flows into the husband
flows into the wife.
When her eyes are closed
she sees him in the water-bird that
leaves no track
yet never forgets the way.
When he is away from her he is still
with her
in the mountain stream running
down to the sea.

NAMELESS PETALS

The final chapters of my life pile up
on one another.
I am overtaken by age
and its attendant mortality.
I know it in my bones
that the central defining reality of
my life and its particulars
is my life with Morris,
the children we raised,
events we shared,
parties we gave
notwithstanding the mistakes
we made together and alone.
Memories are worksheets
scribbled over
and the years are page proofs
corrected or not.
Memories stretch the truth.
stretch the meanings
in the late autumn of my life
(remembering and not remembering)
as the blue of the moon drips
into the landscape
and joy, like a flower, waits
with thousands of nameless
petals to be born.

REFLECTIONS

A SIGN POINTS TO THE SINAGOGIA

A sign points to the *sinagogia*
in the *judiaria.*
If you can find the town of Tomar
in Spain
and can travel there
you'll come upon a white-walled
building.
The *bima* is still standing.
An ark with Torah scrolls leans
against the wall.
A few ancient artifacts are in the room
including a strange old stone
with incised Hebrew letters
700 years old.

The *mikveh*, the ritual bath,
is buried in the ground,
a fitting epilogue to a ruthless
reign of terror
against the Spanish Jews who were
tortured
to force them to convert
to Catholicism.

The *sinagogia* is the legacy of the
Marranos, the *hidden* Jews
in late-medieval Spain
who adhered to Judaism
and practiced their faith secretly
in the darkness of envy and hatred
against them by those
who were jealous of their prominence
in the professions-- in medicine,
literature, philosophy, music
banking and commerce
where they contributed so much to the
culture of Spain
and to the Renaissance.

During the Spanish Inquisition
the forced conversions,
torture and death of thousands
of Jews was ordered by
Pope Innocent VIII and the Church
at the request of Queen Isabella
and Tomas de Torquemada, her Confessor,
her right-hand man and Chief
Inquisitor.

The deaths of thousands of Jews
was designed by the Church
to be carried out in the most gruesome
way
with great pomp and ceremony
as though being burned at the stake
were part of a presentation
in a theater.

The public was invited to watch
the *performance*,
the final scene in the last act of
the drama of forced conversion.
Jews who refused to deny their faith
who remained unbroken in spirit
were tied to a stake.
As the flames licked their bodies
they died reciting the *Shema*:
Hear, O Israel, the Lord our God,
the Lord is One.

For more than 300 years the fires
of the Inquisition burned bright
yet thousands of Jews refused to
renounce their faith.
They remained Jews secretly.
They were the Marranos,
the *hidden* Jews.
Thousands of converted Jews
together with Jews who refused

to deny their Jewish faith
died in the flames of the
Inquisition.

Pope Innocent VIII finally ordered
the Jews expelled from Spain.
The edict of expulsion was signed
by King Ferdinand and Queen Isabella.
Thousands of Jews fled from Spain
to Portugal where, unbeknown
to them,
a worse fate awaited them.
Many thousands of Jews were forcibly
baptized.
Many were sold into slavery.
Others sought escape in death.
Years later, many *hidden* Jews fled to
Holland
and a number of other countries
in Europe.

A surprising number of Marranos
who escaped to Amsterdam
were priests and monks.
Some of them had achieved
great influence in the church.
They asked to be reunited with
their Jewish brothers.
Fra Vicente de Rocamora,
a Dominican friar returned to
Judaism,
assumed the name of Isaac
and spent the rest of his life
as a doctor who practiced medicine.
Many converted Jews also returned
to the faith of their fathers.

Some *hidden* Jews kindled
a new flame
and like the light of a candle

in broad daylight,
many years later they found
freedom in America.
They built the Spanish-Portuguese
synagogue in New York
Their descendants attend
services there today.

If you should visit Spain some day
get out a map
and look for the town of Tomar.
If you get there a sign will point
the way to the *sinagogia*
in the *judiaria*.
When you are in Tomar
You'll come across a white-walled
building.
The *bima* is still in it.
An ark with Torah scrolls still leans
against a wall.
Some ancient artifacts will still be there
including an ancient stone 700 years old
with deeply carved Hebrew letters.

WHERE IS THAT PLACE, SHACKLED TO THE MOON

Where is that place, shackled to the moon,
a place with an aura of light shooting up
into the night sky,
a place where smoking volcanoes rise
on restless, tectonic plates?
Where is that place between the instant
and the duration
that slips off the edge of time
with the sculptural fluidity of water,
the place where Zeus still comes to Danae
in a shower of gold
and a tower of sculpture and light
is borne
through the streets in broad daylight,
the crowd, urging it on?

Where is that place where the moments that stay
with us
determine, ultimately, who we become,
that place that allows us to restructure our
lives,
that place of possibilities beyond what was
first imagined,
that magical place, dark, forested,
smelling of earth and plants,
where confusions are resolved and transformations
take place,
that place where messages are picked up
from the past
even though the time is gone and the past,
irretrievable.

Where is that place where the sun throws light
on the ocean
and the wild ocean laps at the foot of the
shifting tides

and our hearts pound with the urgency
to speak?
Where is that place in which we can create
any future we want,
a place where no meanings are lost
but some meanings don't matter
any more.
Where is that place where love, speaking
without words,
positions her head
on the flat round pillow of the moon?

I AM HOLDING FAST TO AN
INSUBSTANTIAL MOMENT

I am holding fast to an insubstantial moment
with its evanescent air,
but it wants to move into
another dimension
like brush strokes on a canvas
transforming themselves into redemptive
art.

The moment is like seeing a charismatic,
ageless man
waiting in the street,
glimpsed from the window of
an elevated train,
a disturbing vision of unattainable
love
both real and imagined.

It is like holding the word
whisper,
the velvet soft shape of it
in your hand
in a floating world of water and sand
where lines intersect and vanish
with indecent haste.
If you blink your eyes you miss it.

IN THE ATTIC OF MY DARKNESS

I put down a foot, not knowing where.
I stare mutely into my own darkness.
Out come the lame, the children
with swollen bellies, the old, the sick.
the dispossessed of the world.
I lean on my elbows and stare.
The clowns, the misfits, the grotesques
stream over to the secret trap-door
in the attic of my darkness,
a pushing, shoving mob.
A group of musicians crouches,
bending over their instruments.
The violinist tears his bow across
the strings.
The orchestra plays and plays
without stopping.
A shofar blasts its piercing notes.

RIDING THE DEATH CAR

Before you died, mother, you tried to talk to me.
What was it you wanted to say
but couldn't,
entombed in the edematous rooms of your
lungs?
In the house of your body with its boarded up
windows
the water rose.
After your escape I traveled down that
underground tunnel
where whole trainloads vanished
riding the death car with the six pointed star.

THE MESSIAH OF DEATH

I listen to the rattle of your breath
lapping against water.
Around me time hangs motionless
and dumb.
Ani-Ma'amin! Still I believe
with perfect faith in the coming of
the messiah, the messiah
of Death!
Even though he tarry, yet will he come!

Now you lie dead.
Lora and I wash you and dress you
for burial.

Rachel lifts the gravedigger's shovel
to cover you with earth.
Again I live through the night of your
dying.
Weaned from you I labor for syllables.
My anguish gives birth.

Oh, little mother, *Lo amut ki ehyeh!*
I shall not die (with you)
but live!
In my head lie galaxies of poems.
Praise be to that maw in which oceans roll
their fish.
Praise be to the dark erection of the penis
of thought.
Praise be to the blue bloom on the bulging
uterus of life!

REQUIEM FOR A VANISHED DREAM

The sun is setting behind a railroad track.
An immensely long train is rushing by.
Its ominous cry pierces
the silence.
The ground under my feet
shakes hard like the beginning
of an earthquake.

I look into the windows of
the passenger cars
searching for one familiar face,
seized by a wild longing
I do not understand.
"Take me with you!" I implore.
The train speeds on.

After it has passed from sight
my eyes frame an empty space
which might be sky, earth, a tree
or a train of thought
with its sacred, sexual, beautiful
efflorescence
and its willingness to be
my new life devoted to
incarnational labor.

REQUIEM FOR A VANISHED PLACE

A Purple Fountain weeps copper Beech.
The weeping Hemlock is juxtaposed
with the Purple Fountain
for dramatic effect.
And above these trees is an infinite
ocean of sky frothing with universes.
On the ground the reddening Sumac
throws its wide shadow across
the track.
As the sun sets a train flies past
the grade crossing.
I shade my eyes from the sun's
direct rays
and peer through the windows of
the railroad cars.
The train is hauling its cargo
of dreams
to a place unreachable--
a destination and a destiny.

FIRMLY ROOTED IN THE DIVINE SPIRIT

What would you say if darkness shifted
as if it were a liquid?
You who bear the seed of the future
within yourself
do you see yourself as already
posthumous,
firmly rooted in the divine Spirit
even in death?

How do you uncreate yourself?
And how do you imagine a time when
you can no longer imagine--
when you are a poet of nothing?
People say to be a visionary
is to be a holy fool
and the mystics say that prayer is
copulation with the *Shekinah*.

A BUSH AFLAME

Time has abandoned the green places
in the wilderness.
The desert oases are gone with their wells.
Only an empty pitcher remains.
In the virile, deep-in-the-throat language
of Hebrew
the Holy One wanders in the desert of
my soul.
He raises high a luminous scroll
on which are written hermetic words,
strange and prophetic:
"O tempest-tossed, irreconcilable one,
see to it that all your actions are a Torah
and that you, yourself, become entirely
a Torah.
Only then will you be whole."

I argue with the *Shekhina*, the feminine
aspect of God:
How can I become the bearer of
God's word--
I, lost in a wilderness of words?
What trick is this--
to live my life's authenticity and
essence
like a blazing fire, a bush aflame
yet not consumed,
writing at top speed and then
perish
like Moses who, in his old age,
was forbidden to enter the
Promised Land
and knew no rest until he died
of God's kiss!

THE UNIVERSE IS A MASSIVE, MONUMENTAL POEM

The universe is a massive, monumental poem
constantly transforming itself.
Words, like stars, are the dangerous possessors
of occulted powers
and like art, itself, unimaginable without
risk.
Something deeply hidden is behind things
leaving marks like an ancient alphabet
written by a diviner who travels through space
and then is gone.

THE COSMIC GAZE INWARD

I am sitting in a cafe on Bleeker Street
furtively thinking the unthinkable--
those fugitive thoughts that refuse
to be put on paper.

Do all past events exist simultaneously?
Is time a circular space?
When the circular line opens and separates
is there freedom to begin anywhere
on the curve?

Shall I deconstruct historical truth
made up of half-truths and lies?
Or transform and displace old scenes
and events
from the shifting waters of the past?

Like an ocean vessel riding low in
those waters I can see below
what has darkened me as a poet
and deepened me as a woman.

THE UBIQUITOUS MUSE

Life is the flesh of the moment
my Muse declares
as she stalks through my life
alluringly thin
skin pressing closer and closer
to skin.
It's no secret that I envy her
her proud walk
her spirited talk
her lashes like pendants
raking over me.
Her passion erupts
like the explosion of Krakatoa.
With her feather boa
her streaming hair
shoulder-scraping earrings
her black dress and pearls
she whirls around me.
Together we dance a *pas de deux*.
I hold in my arms an infant wrapped
in a prayer shawl.
I lift him high
for everyone to see
as though he were a Torah scroll,
the little *tzaddik*.

"Something unknown is doing
I don't know what!"[1]
I am wearing a *kippah*,
eight threads and six knots.
Angels appear in a sky daubed
with numbers and signs.
The Muse paints the stars blue
to ward off the evil eye.
She drops seeds of new life
into the Big Dipper.
Light breaks in a stellar explosion
creating islands of stillness

from which souls fly
to human beings
part breath, part smoke.
Signs and letters drift dreamlike
in a transforming vision
where two are three
and three are one
in the Kabbalah
whose first language is
poetry.

PARCHMENTS AND TORAH SKINS

Words are parchments rescued from the flames.
They are Torah skins retrieved from floodwaters.

Like the effulgent light of Hebrew letters
they cling to life.

I am awed by the mystery of the Word colored by
the Jewish mission in history.

I lift my hands high like an Old Testament prophet
who gestures, prays, supplicates and waits

under an El Greco sky.

THE HEBREW LETTERS OF THE ALPHABET

The Hebrew letters of the alphabet
cast an endless spell over me
like the letters of my Hebrew name
Hannah
which reads the same backwards
or forwards.
From the letters of my name that
shattered like crystal
and came together again stronger
than ever, they are, by turns,
voluptuous and ascetic.
The letters are part of the drama
of events
still unfolding in real time
in life and death.
The letters of Hannah's name
are bewildered,
unable to find peace and caring
in a world at war with itself.
I grieve for humanity.

THE HOURGLASS

I am wreathed in flowering yellow
scrolls
where the new and the unexpected
are interposed.
I speak to the turmoil of my time--
wars raging in the Middle East
from the seeds of enormous
disruptive forces.
"I gather stray phrases into
strings of thought."[1]
They catch sparks from no visible
flame.
I hold an hourglass in my hand
and carefully shake the sand
for a few grains of truth.

THE LETTERS OF THE ALPHABET OF LOVE

The letters of the alphabet of love pummeled
by the strokes of fate

The syllables of the word of God twisted
in the mouth of the Serpent

The pleading sounds of the shofar calling me

Elijah's wine cup filled with longing and hope

Stones crying out from the Western Wall

Great waves of birds at the limits of sound

A bloody pebble flung up from the sea

All the unfree people of the world weeping
for truth, conscience and freedom.

PROFOUNDLY CONNECTED

Grandpa, the Hasid, traveled every year
to a distant city in Russia to visit
his beloved rabbi.
Is that why I, also, set out on
journeys of the spirit?

My grandpa's God was a God
of wandering
a God of journeying
a God of the Land
who fleshed out the moral code
with *Remember* and *Keep--*
with the warm pressure of
his hand.

He explored the arcana of
the Talmud and the Kabbalah
and like Jacob, he, too,
wrestled with an angel.
Prayer was his pilgrimage.
Poetry is mine.

REMAINING STEADFAST

Ecclesiastes teaches there is a time
for everything
but what happens to us is ultimately
bashert.[1]
Well, yes and no.
When we are swept off balance by
events of the day
are we able to maintain
our moral compass
in a world that is part Kafka
and part Carnivale?
Yes! Yes! But everything passes.
Things change.
All things in our lives unite
and press forward
while Big God watches with His
inexhaustible eyes.

THE MOON IS A LEADEN BALL

The moon is a leaden ball tied to a
prisoner's foot

The prisoner is condemned to drag it
along from horizon to horizon.

Suddenly the path of the sky forks.
Which way should the moonlight go?

WHAT WOULD BEETHOVEN HAVE SAID?

What would Beethoven have said
if he had known tens of thousands of
musicians, writers, artists, actors
and dancers would be brutally tortured
and put to death
because they were Jews?
What would Beethoven have done
if he had lived during the takeover of
Germany and Austria by Hitler
and the Nazi party?
How would he have reacted to the
round-ups, the death camps,
the murder of millions of Europe's Jews
and millions of soldiers and civilians
caught up in World War II?
Would he have emigrated to England
or America?
Would he still have composed
his Ninth Symphony with its outsized
vision of the brotherhood of all men?
Would he have been able to say
about freedom in the largest sense,
"You millions I embrace you!"

HOLLOWED OUT BY CHISELS OF FIRE

The sky is thundery and brooding.
Gnarled with age, a venerable old tree
with its pendulous branches provides
enlightenment.
In piney woods the stump of an old
tree is still standing,
a defiant stump hollowed out by
chisels of fire.

Who can rest on the bank of a river
that knows no rest?
Who is sitting in holy water in a
bathtub in a junkyard?
Who resurrects poems from the
ash-heap of death?
Who molds words and phrases with
her hands
"like clay in the hands of a potter"?[1]
Who knows that losing tears
and blood by turns is accompanied
by the music of pots and pans?

THE WORLD'S BIRTHDAY

God remembered Sarah on Rosh Hashanah.
Isaac was born on Rosh Hashanah.
Hannah was remembered on Rosh Hashanah.
All who were part of me
before they died
I remember on Rosh Hashanah
but my yesterdays will not come back.
Death demolished their physical bodies.
Death uproots.
Tyrants murder innocent people.
Tattered stars are still crushed
with eyeglasses.
What kind of birthday is this
for the world?

AS THE SUN IS REDUCED TO A CINDER

Is Preposterella putting on her virginal nightgown
or getting decked out in the naughty red dress
of her fantasies?
Her irony is what makes her deepest meaning
bearable.
She calls out to a black-crowned night heron
glimpsed in flight.
The bird doesn't recognize her.
She is swollen with life on top of the piano,
under it, embracing it.
Preposterella dips bells into holy water.
She sees a faunlike creature perched in a tree
playing the flute.
She sees a flower that won't allow itself
to be taken.
She sees, looming up, the scaffold where
her words were regularly flogged and executed.
She sees a bell that did not go unpunished.
It was taken down, carted through the streets,
whipped and sent into exile.
Piano chords crash in the air.
She cradles the keyboard in her arms.
The burnt sun rises over the hills.
A rose blooms from a pile of ashes.
Preposterella takes a dead butterfly
in the palms of her hands,
blows on it with her warm breath
until the wings loosen.
The frail butterfly staggers
into the air.

THE MAN WITHOUT ANY SKIN

One day I met a man without any skin.
He was sitting in a litter of old paint tubes
and discarded canvases in an alley
of rocks.
His ideas were strange, yet oddly
familiar.
He painted with unabashed
expansiveness
before retreating back into the darkness
of the alley.

Although he grew steadily more sure
of himself
he sank deeper into the remoteness
in which he lived.
Sometimes a painting would occupy him
for months, even years.
He repainted certains canvases more than
a hundred times
yet there was a spontaneity, a freshness
about them.

The art critics took note of his work
but were unaware that in his paintings
voices were weeping, erased from history.
They rejected his work and compared it
to the contents of a garbage can
transformed into a ritual offering.
The man without any skin was chilled
to the bone.
He continued to drag his paintbrush
through dense pigment.
Every day he painted, scraped the paint off,
painted and repainted the same surface again
and again.

The canvas began to glow with encrusted pigment
in a liquid field of crystallized stones.

In the last painting the artist framed before he died,
a face emerged in the half-light,
an ashen face shifting and amorphous
against a smoking background.
It gazed sadly through the wires of a fence.

After his death, critics who had denigrated his work
established its relevance in the history of art.
As in Cezanne's final paintings
and Beethoven's last piano sonatas and
string quartets,
the artist without any skin reached beyond
the origin of things and their meanings.
He focused his gaze of unblinking intensity
on colors that had been sitting around his palette
for years
that were now spread out across the canvas.

Art museums began to outbid each other
in an effort to acquire his paintings.
They mounted exhibitions and retrospectives
all over the country.
He gave his inner life a form, a narrative,
a timeless chronology.
His last canvases embraced the effort
to express the formless and the unknowable
still to come to light on earth
and in the cosmos.

IN A CAVE AT THE MOUTH OF THE SEA OF REEDS

In a cave at the mouth of the sea of reeds
waves lashed the rocks.
I gave birth in the cave to a hairy animal
covered with seaweed.
Its prehensile tail was twisted around
its legs.
Its voluptuous body and sensuous lips
(it was full-grown)
were an embarrassment to me.
I did not know how to talk to it.
It spoke in the language of dolphins
and whales.
How was I to give it the love
it craved?

I was still in mourning for the death
of color.
I was dressed in black.
My lipstick was black.
Then the creature and I connected with
the saturated blue of the sky.
A euphoric fountain shot high in the air
like the great fountains of Rome.
The prehistoric animal began to sing
in shifting registers.
Her voice vibrated like a tuning fork.
She held notes past the vanishing point.
She dressed herself in a riot of color.
She wore a feather boa around her shoulders.
She wore high-heeled shoes.
She is convinced she is my Muse.
What am I to do?
She is steadfast and unapologetic.
Together we face the ultimate Unknowability
of it all.

MANY THREADS

I spin my life into a fabric
of love.
In the fabric is a crossing
of many threads.
I pull the threads of love
and desire
out of a ragbag of myth
revealing moments of ecstasy
locked in orgiastic embrace
throughout my life.
A modest portion of legend
remains.
I open the pages of the last
chapters of my life.
As my last days draw near
I empty out my art
and give everything away
in gratitude for all that was
and is.
For all that is yet to be
thank you, God.

ON THE DEATH OF MY BROTHER

There is no language for my thoughts
try as I might to follow my brother's
night journey
to the aura of the other side.
I can only live on this side of silence.
When my brother died
a seraph opened my eyes and ears
and tore out my tongue and my heart.
I run my head up against the limits
of language
where the undercurrents of silence
flow.
The mystery of his death remains
looming like an obelisk over his grave
which is still open.

FROM THE BOOK OF ANTICIPATIONS

This moment has never happened before.
Let it be fruitful and multiply.

It exists like a deep and startling blue
gay with flowers blooming fiercely.

Like sunlight shining through a prism
of glass

it is spinning rainbows on the floor.

It carries no memories of yesterday
or the day before.

It carries on its back a load of the souls
of those still waiting to be born.

GREAT WOMEN IN THE OLD TESTAMENT

Eve, mother of us all, was hungry
and thirsty for knowledge.
After God expelled Eve and Adam
from the Garden of Eden
she gave birth to generations
of extraordinary women--
to Miriam, the prophet, daughter of
Yocheved,
sister of Moses and Aaron
who led the women in song and dance
after crossing the Red Sea
in the exodus from Egypt,
to Huldah, prophet and teacher
and Deborah, military leader,
wise judge and prophet
whose words, like Huldah's, were
recorded in Scriptures.

Eve was the progenitor, the foremother
of the four Matriarchs:
Sarah, Rebecca, Rachel and Leah.
They, in turn, were embraced by
the *Shekhina*, the feminine aspect
of God,
the Holy-One-Who-Dwells-in-This-World,
creator of all souls.

Women living in the 21st century:
we have our own genesis
through which we must pass.
Inscribe the word *Shaddai*[1]
upon the doorposts of your houses
and upon your gates.
Be strong and proud of your biblical
heritage.
May the extraordinary accomplishments
of women in ages past

turn every rock into a fountain of
love
and be a lightning rod of hope
pointing the way forward
as we live our lives with courage,
dignity, wisdom and compassion.

OCTOBER SONG

REBIRTH OF THE GARDEN

A timpani of newly planted bulbs
thumps emphatically underground.
The garden clears its throat and sings
Das Lied von der Erde
followed by the operatic roses
Ferdinand Pichard and Fair Bianca
singing arias
from *Tristan und Isolde*
above a chorus of bleeding hearts.
Lilies in the corps de ballet
whirl *en pointe*.
Red tulips startle and challenge
the delphiniums, enduringly
hopeful.
Daffodils open their mouths
and hit a high C.
Birds of Paradise, unable to fly,
offer libations and kisses toward
the ground.
Orchids dance on bushes and trees.
New blossoms open.
Flames of color meet, part
and reunite.
The garden is ablaze.

THE FLOWERS COME ALIVE AT NIGHT

The flowers come alive at night
in a tangle of assumed names
and identities
like the characters in Mozart's
comic operas.
If you could hear them sing
summoning outpourings of sound
unabashedly passionate
holding nothing back
exposing and celebrating
their hungers and dreams
creating unforgettable scenes
the music would be so deafening
so overwhelming
so viscerally exciting
you would suspend your disbelief.

NEAR THE LIMITS OF HEARING

The garden is not silent.
The fuchia shakes out her wrinkled skirts
smacking her lips.
The big scarlet poppy forces open her sepals
with a sudden "plock."
Irises in labor sigh triumphantly.
Flowers are slaves of their sexuality.
Tormented by dark thoughts
some have savage and unpredictable caprices.

With a tickling and a shudder
the gentle butterwort folds her hairy leaf
over her victim.
The climbing pea strikes like a python's head.
In the midst of her fevered life
the Venus Flytrap snaps her hinged mandibles
and devours her prey.
A scented climber known as the Cruel Plant
sets its sticky traps for pollinating moths,
holding them by their probosces.

The sump of the birthwort is filled
with victims.
Behind the cannibal sounds of flowers
that devour,
lilies with their tall stamens
and blobs of fluffy pollen
share themselves with honeybees
that show a priapic alertness.
The shock of surprise brings up large
subversive thoughts about gardens
(wildly improvisational)
and insects that morph into flowering
plants.

THE GARDEN IS STEEPED IN THE PERFUME
OF OLD ROSES

The Garden is steeped in the perfume of
old roses
and golden foliage in autumn.
It speaks softly from its stones, mounds
and paths.
I listen to the splash of water and the singing
of the wind.
The garden is a fragile vision,
a symbiosis between gardener and garden.
It cannot exist without exchanges:
the bond is indestructible.
The garden gives and it receives,
but while it reflects its creator
it also pursues its own life.
It has the capacity, the tenacity,
the audacity to flower late.

THE FIRES OF MID-OCTOBER ARE BREAKING OUT

The fires of mid-October are breaking out
among the azaleas, red dahlias
and Celosia plumosa.
Flames are rising in the Japanese maples.
Young birches are turning yolk-yellow,
the middle-aged conifers burnt umber
and the aging trees dead leaf brown.
A heavy frost descends.
Gathering shadows appear, soft
and indistinct.
Smoke rises in the distant hills.
I walk through the valley of falling
leaves
as I stretch out my hands toward the glow
of an unseen fire.

OCTOBER SONG

In spring and summer you fought hard
to make your garden safe
from predators
but in late fall nature has outlasted
all your efforts.
Your flower arrangements are laid low
but there are new bursts of color--
dark reds, lusty oranges and full-throated
yellows brightening each day.
Still, the garden is winding down
even as new combinations of colors
are forming, if only for a short time
in the hazy sunlight.

IN LATE OCTOBER THERE COMES AN END TO RIOTOUS COLOR

In late October there comes an end
to riotous color.
The wind slices through the trees
like a knife.
Arthritic leaves fall one by one.
The stiff, papery leaves move
in a continuous thread of dance
before the sun goes down.
Trees have the gift of letting go.
Leaves know when to fall off
instead of clinging to trees.
Trees respond to their own internal
rhythm
that answers in a way only leaves
understand.
Each leaf is a bold exclamation point
in a stream of dying leaves.

The pace of the falling quickens.

WORK IN THE GARDEN IS NEVER COMPLETED

Work in the garden is never completed.
There is always another seed to plant,
another blossom to pluck.
The garden is constantly evolving--
poetic and spiritual made manifest.
If you tame it, it is an ordered paradise.
If you harmonize with it, it is a
natural paradise.
Each bud ultimately translates into
a flower having the potential to represent
more than itself.
With so much potential available,
what does the garden want
as the season draws to a close
and a huge inky blot of a cloud falls on
the landscape?
It wants a simple, orderly, meditative
existence
and time and space to reflect.

MISCELLANEOUS

WHAT IS THERE TO SAY ABOUT THE WAY TIME USES ME?

What is there to say about the way time uses me?
It tells me there are rocks to break
a road to pave
sand to excavate.
It says I must return
to the sand
to the road
to the ditch
and to the bricks.
It forces me to run a gauntlet of straps and whips.

It plows backwards in the furrows of my mind.
It repeats my days and nights along the long road
of dying and death.
It flies over enchanted Vitebsk
with a noose to strangle the lovers and a hook
to drag them.
Do you understand what time is doing?
It offers me poison with one hand
and an antidote with the other.

Time tells me time and time again
there are rocks to break
a road to pave
sand to excavate.
It says I must return
to the sand
to the road
to the ditch
and to the bricks
watched over by *Samael*, the angel
of death.

A SINGLE WORD OPEN TO CHANCE

Emmet is wearing the simplicity of
the one robe.
He recites the Sutra of the one
word.
So many years of trying to fit into
so many robes,
so many robes, so many textures,
so many colors.
The word throws out a language
that makes whole the pieces
of the universe.
A single word open to chance.

THOUGHTS OF A RED EMPRESS IN THE LAOTSE-CHUANGTSE ERA BASED ON HER EXPERIENCES

The Red Empress sat on her Throne of Sapphires
for ninety-three years.
The clouds of heaven dropped diamonds and gold
before thickening.
The marble trees rained yellow leaves.
The Red Empress contemplated the mystery of
the softest substance going through the hardest.
She meditated on that-which-has-no-crevice
in the great space that has no corners.
Then the Empress rose from her Throne of Sapphires
declaring to all:
I am drunk with color. I am drunk with sound.
Debauchery in color! Debauchery in sound!
Yet the climax of my actions remains in my head,
unbearably deferred
like a peach or a pear stuck fast in a tree,
unwilling to fall into anyone's hands
for in this life, to be united is to be parted
and to be completed is to be destroyed.

MEDITATION ON A QUIET NIGHT

I will take you to the Sea of Green Light
and you will take me to the Mountain
of Yang.
I will lead you through the Door of
Many Changes
and you will walk with me through the
Valley of Yin
and I will show you how one candle
that has fallen over
still burns without destroying life
around it.

Together we will climb to the top
of Jacob's Ladder
interwoven with golden thread.
There Time is without any interval.
We will rejoice in that Place
and read the Kabbalah and the Zohar
and embrace the Torah
with its head, heart, mouth
and soul
as it scrolls and twists,
rolls and unscrolls.

APPASSIONATO

What is this very tense
and wounding dance of flirtation
between self and Muse?
It is akin to the profoundly bitter chocolate
the Aztecs once sipped,
as unforgettable as black pepper
ice cream,
or the tartness of lemon zest
or the pungency of cumin.
And yes, the dance is like the dark side
of sweetness.

Such is the symbiosis of self and Muse,
this sweet and sour--
welcoming, intrusive, unmanageable.
Impossible to know all the steps
of the dance
while pitting the dizzy sense
of the world's transient splendor
against unbearable silence.

APPASSIONATA SONATA

What shall I do with my imperative need
to communicate
to be touched
to be profoundly connected in the heart?
Writers need someone,
a connection between the validity
of their experiences and the empty page.

A single life can have many biographies
including inadvertent leavings
and expurgations.
We will ourselves to be present
without guilt
in our reincarnations
as we journey
toward the terrifying beauty of
the glass mountain.
Let us fast-forward progress
toward it
or upend it altogether.

THE BITTERNESS OF TIME

I close my eyes, the better to see, to see clearly
while the bitterness of time drips
on the platforms of departing railroad stations.
Time moves ahead like a night watchman
waving a lantern among a jumble of tracks.
I look at the colors of time decomposing
on the walls of my house.
I listen to time falling drop by drop into the sink.
Every surface is a clock-face to be read.
I go on in my steady, sturdy, stodgy, much-worn
thoughts
but in my feelings I stand like a Picasso woman
with three noses and a fish for a hat.

OLD WOMAN IN THE DOCTOR'S OFFICE

Doctor, I sit in silence in your office,
my mask-like face carved in stone.
I shiver with exhaustion.
I cannot see.
I cannot eat.
Silence has calcified my speech
drenched in despair the color
of gallstones.
I am short of breath--
a headless, armless statue,
a broken column.
I, an old woman, expose my body
to your touch.
You poke and probe--
loose flesh a pile of squirmy dough
lips faded and sapless
hairs thin and few.
My thoughts a stew of fears
and confusion.
My hand gripped by the hand
of death.

WHO WILL BELIEVE THIS?

Nothing seems to be steady here.
Things shake and drop
in this place I've come to.
It's called: Old Age.
Suddenly I'm there!
The roadside is strewn with casualties
but I, I've made it alive.
Finally, I. too, am carried off
accompanied by mourners supporting
each other.
Look, they're crying now.
The gravediggers are planting my coffin,
lowering it with straps.
If they plant me too shallow
I will freeze in winter
and cook in summer.
If they plant me too deep
how will my soul push up to new heights?
I am in a daze.
Who will believe this?
I refuse to accept what is happening
but how can I live in a world
where babies in prams gobble up
old ladies?

HELFGOTT IN AVERY FISHER HALL

The performance began with his entry
from the wings.
He came bounding out with boyish
exuberance
in a triumphant return to the concert
stage after his derailed career
as a concert pianist.
His fans gave him an ecstatic welcome.
Those seated in the front rows
of Avery Fisher
overheard his whispered conversations
with himself.
His octaves were lean and incisive
fierce and vigorous.
Melodies flew up and down the keys
in rising and falling *glissandos*
creating delicate ripples of sound
in "La Campanella".
Helfgott, the pianist, was liberated,
unbound.
When the last note of the music
died down
he hurried to the footlights
and extended his arms in a wide
embrace.
He gifted the audience with his
unselfconscious charm,
his ineffable smile
and the courage it took for this
risk-taking artist to perform
at Lincoln Center
after years of psychotic illness.

TO THE FALCONER

You have to let the peregrine falcon go.
She must not return to you once she
flies away.
She is learning how to be on her own.
You must learn, too.
Let her fly off.
Her future is not with you.
It is with other falcons
who understand flight patterns
and the magnetic pull of sun, moon
and stars.
She's at home with earth lights,
clouds scudding by
and the wind blowing with ferocious
speed.
She flies above your head
with outstretched wings beating firmly.
Let her fly free.
Don't call her back.
She isn't yours.

SWIMMING UPSTREAM

The humpbacked salmon is tired of leaping
over waterfalls
and swimming upstream against the current.
Already she is dull-colored and soft
but her implacable will moves her on--
two thousand miles up the Yukon.
Blotches of fungus creep down her back.
Her fins are ragged, she is full of rot
but she tries to make it to the spawning place
to deposit her eggs before she dies.
The sacrifice repeats itself
from salmon to salmon.
A salmon is sometimes eaten alive
by bears foraging in the river
for food after hibernating all winter.
Some salmon do not stay alive long enough
to deposit their eggs.
Such is the uncertainty of life
and the possibility of loss.
The salmon will continue to swim upstream
against all odds
that she will survive the strangely familiar
landscape of death
and be able to deposit her eggs
in a safe place.

BABY SEAL HARVEST

While seagulls wheel and fly about
the clubbers approach the seals
with a shout.
They move in for the kill with clubs
that resemble baseball bats.
The baby seals huddle together.
The clubs rain down blow
upon blow.
The clubbers finish off hundreds
of seals.
They drag the bodies into long lines
to fill tallies of ten.
The slitters make cuts around the
flippers.
Quickly they jerk loose each pelt.
Many baby seals are skinned alive.
Each white pelt is peeled off
like a warm glove
and thrust on the ground to cool.
A new crew of workers arrives
in Diesel trucks.
They mop up the dead seals,
pitching the cold skins in one truck,
the carcasses in another.
The baby seal hunt is over.
Those who question the sealers
about the pain inflicted
on baby seals that are clubbed
to death
have a ready answer.
They tell you
it doesn't mean anything.
What it looks like is not what it is.
"Seals are not human,"
they insist.
"It's just an honest day's work."

IN THE YEAR 3000 A.D.

Who shall make the choices
for lucidity and order?
for population control?
for sperm banks and host mothers?
Who shall be cloned and who shall not
for a breed of superior fighters?
for a caste of subservient workers?
Who shall be responsible for babies
in hatcheries?
Who shall control the artificial wombs?
Who shall supervise fertilized eggs?
Who shall take memory pills?
Who shall be given transplantation of
brain cells
and from whom shall be taken the long
reaches of the past?
Does there exist for each a limit?
The proportions and rhythms of life are
askew:
the arrangements of society
environmental depredation
the deranged views of world leaders
obsessed metaphysicians
social acquisitions
politicians embracing lies
disguised as truths.
What delirious geometry can measure
the uses put to human genetic lines and
properties based on theorems?
How can the soul of things shine through?
Most importantly,
can people live again with the full
understanding of what it means
to be human?

STONE THOUGHTS

Earth's seas and lakes wear their shores away. People live in symbols to survive. Dictators, like huge magnets, suck up the innocent, trample their identities, invade other countries with bullets and lies.

The biblical hills offer no comfort. The wind sings among spasms of dust like a flute full of water. The trampled grass struggles to live.

Faith collapses, gray and unconscious. Statues tumble from their niches and break. The gods keep multiplying. They reproduce and reinvent themselves.

Chimneys belch with infernal indigestion. The gods are hungry. The graves are full. Shadows spread over the mournful grass. The statues return to their niches.

New deities rise. The ultimate adultery: lying to the people. Truth cut off at the knees. A coffin for the body of truth. New iconic gods sing off-key. Power reinforced with hypnotic glue. Catalogued, numbered people. Corrupt governments. The world falling into a black hole of warring factions.

Nuclear dementia. Warheads skyrocketing. Competing gods riding waves of technology. The smoke, the debris, the ash. Humankind reduced to quarks and leptons.

Books cooked. A rhetoric of shock and awe. Desperation travels through moody terrain.

Earth crosses night with its little lightening floating in ten-dimensional space. Piles of discarded circuit boards. Cell phones and computers burning. The trees veneered in black ebony.

Can we take back the non-fictionalized view of life that wars reveal in air attacks, infrastructures torn apart and in collateral damage? We cannot avoid the inescapable fact of our own mortality. Is it too late for a quiet, soaring epiphany?

THE VILLAGERS' STORY
Sar Cheshma, Afghanistan 10/96

The Tajik villagers are eager to tell
how their village died,
how it was shelled and burned
and how the smell of torched ruins
hung heavy in the air.

Taliban fighters swept in at dawn,
poured canisters of gasoline
into courtyard houses
and set them on fire, wiping out
the whole village.

They described how the fighters ran
between fire-blackened houses
as they rushed to board trucks
that carried them away
from the sacking of Sar Cheshma.

Little remains now except bed frames
and melted kitchen utensils.
The turbaned warriors of
the Taliban
destroyed everything in sight.

In the charred ruins, a villager sifts
through his blackened grain
hoping to find enough uncharred
grain
to carry away.

In a rush of grief the grain is
forgotten
as he rescues the ashes of his
beloved Koran,
a book that was in his family
for generations.

The villager shouts out loud:
This is God's book!
Why didn't I die instead of
my book?
Weeping, he carries the cold ashes
of his bible in a bowl.

A village woman cries out:
I refuse to flee.
My husband was killed fighting
in Kabul
but the fighting follows me.

Whatever portion of my life remains
I will live it here
for places are not just buildings
in space.
They are emotional presences.

SOMEONE ELSE'S SON ROCKS SILENTLY

Someone else's son rocks silently
on his heels.
Someone else's daughter lies underground
in the killing fields.

The grieving villagers return to Srebrenica,
surveying the ruins.
The remains of babies are littered about,
frozen on the ground.

Retreating soldiers taunt the villagers.
This is God's revenge, they shout.
Heathens! Unbelievers!
God, Himself, has punished you.

HOW MANY DARK AND DESPERATE DAYS OF DOWNPOUR

How many dark and desperate days of downpour
will continue to fall
from these threatening skies?
I remember how the village echoed at night
with shrieks and cries.
People heard them but were afraid to help.
We cleaned up all the prisoners
but I did not get rich from the shootings
and lootings.
I am poor and without work.
My children are hungry.

I was silent about this for a long time
for I expected someone in my country
would praise me for my courage.
Single-handedly, I killed scores of people,
nine of them women.
Others were rewarded with sumptuous houses
and a good life
but I returned from Vukovar without a *kuna*
in my pocket.
I obeyed orders. I did my duty.

IN THE CITIES AND MOUNTAINS OF IRAQ

In the cities and mountains of Iraq
black veils of despair drape the land,
the land that was once the biblical
Mesopotamia.
Let some great Ulysses of the mind
kill fear with its hulk of serpents.
Who dares to cut off the head of Medusa
with her deadly stare?
This generation also slays its monsters
but where, oh, where is the Golden Fleece?
Our soldiers captured Saddam Hussein,
the Chimera of Iraq.
Still misery abounds.
Misery is boundless.
Misery spreads itself over the land.
Suicide bombers blow themselves up
and take countless innocent people
with them,
They blow themselves up in mosques,
marketplaces,
hotels, even in wedding receptions,
and at funerals.
Soldiers are killed by roadside bombs.
Fortune's cards are shuffled
and reshuffled.
Danger is everywhere.
Hatred and anger stalk the land.
God's eyes are like a giant electronic
camera with a billion pixels.
What do His eyes see?
They see aerial bombardment.
They see fires burning.
They see torture chambers.
They see the Marines in Ramadi,
American infantry in Baghdad.
They see wrecked Humvees
fighting in Kirkuk, Mosul
and Falluja.

They see the karmic wind stirring up
a storm.
They see the insurgency growing,
gaining strength
and the fragile Iraqi government
on the brink of civil war.

A LONG TIME AGO, A FAR-AWAY COUNTRY DOOMED ITSELF

A long time ago, a far-away country doomed itself
to isolation and decay.
It carried a guilt that could not be expiated.
The people were neither dismayed nor shocked
into taking action against their countrymen
who blind-sided the country.
They went about as though nothing had happened
for they, too, were informers and torturers
in order to survive.
Only one soldier refused to shoot his neighbors
lined up for execution.
He was transferred from the firing squad
to the line of victims.
Evil is rampant in the world.
Every man is capable of coveting
what is not rightfully his and of acting out
his forbidden desires,
given the right circumstances.
If there is no *teshuvah*, no *turning*,
no repentance for crimes of the heart
and for mind-rapes
anyone is capable of shootings, lootings
or murder from within.
If there is no spiritual *turning* in the direction
of kindness, compassion and love
we will die without having made peace
with ourselves--
unshriven, unforgiven.

NOTES

p. 74

[1] Dr. Janusz Korczak, writer and doctor, devoted his life to orphaned children and their rights. Korczak's orphanage did not survive the deportations. The children were ordered to march to the death trains. Korczak resisted every effort of his Polish friends to save him. He amazed frantic deportees and the Polish police with the calm way he led the children onto the train.

p. 83

[1] from the Reconstructionist Foundation Prayer Book (paraphrased)

[2] from Job (paraphrased)

p. 106

[1] 12th century Kabbalist

[2] Solomon's other name

p. 114

[1] Habakkuk

[2] Amos

p. 119

[1] Hebrew for *soul*

[2] Psalm 104:4

p. 121

[1] from Habakkah 2:3

p. 145

[1] from the *Talmud*

p. 154

[1]*Binah* is profound and primal. It is mentioned in the Kabbalah, based on a mystical method of interpreting the Scriptures. The Kabbalah is the heart of Jewish mysticism. *Binah* is an illuminating flash of understanding. In the depths of

278

Binah lies *Hokhamah*, Wisdom. *Binah* is also called *Teshuvah*, Return.

p. 156
> [1] Bible: Deut. 12.23
> [2] Ezekiel 16.6

p. 179
> [1] 13th century Jewish Spanish mystic and Kabbalist

p. 185
> [1] "Save me from the lion's mouth: thou hast heard me also from among the horns of unicorns." --Psalms 22:21
> "Canst thou bind the unicorn with his band in the furrow?" --Book of Job

p. 197
> [1] 13th century Jewish Spanish mystic and Kabbalist

p. 221
> [1] Words spoken by the physicist, Eddington

p. 225
> [1] Solomon Ibn Gabirol (c. 1021-1058), Spanish poet, philosopher, and moralist.

p. 228
> [1] Yiddish: predestined, fated

p. 231
> [1] from the words of an unknown Hebrew poet in a Rosh Hashanah-Yom Kippur prayer

p. 240
> [1] one of the names of God

Printed in the United States
83957LV00002B/247-330/A